God's Hal

Peter Lewis

Christian Focus

ISBN 1 85792 529 7

Published in 1999
by Christian Focus Publications, Geanies House, Fearn, Ross-shire, IV20 1TW, Great Britain. Previously published in 1996 by Hodder & Stoughton with the title *God's Honours List*.

Cover design by Owen Daily

Contents

Introduction		vii
1.	Celebration of Faith	1
2.	Faith Recognising Its Creator	11
3.	Faith Resented and Honoured (Abel)	19
4.	Faith Walking with God (Enoch)	27
5.	Faith and Its Reward	35
6.	Faith Learning to Fear (Noah)	45
7.	Faith Aware of Its Inheritance (Abraham)	53
8.	Faith Grasping the Promises of God (Abraham and Sarah)	63
9.	Faith Looking Forward	71
10.	Faith Tested and Triumphant (Abraham and Isaac)	79
11.	Faith Aware of God's Plan (Isaac, Jacob and Joseph)	87
12.	Faith Making Its Choice (Moses)	97
13.	Faith Taking Shelter in God (Israel and the Passover Lamb)	107
14.	Faith Passing the Point of No Return (Israel at the Red Sea)	115
15.	Faith Aware of God's Power (Joshua and Rahab)	123
16.	Faith Taking Its Opportunities (Barak, Deborah and Jael)	133
17.	Faith Learning to Fight (Gideon)	143
18.	Faith Rising Above Rejection (Jephthah)	153
19.	Faith Learning the Hard Way (Samson)	163
20.	Faith Recovering (Samuel)	171
21.	Faith Gaining Control (David)	179
22.	Faith Losing Control (David)	185
23.	Faith Suffering	193
24.	Faith Looking unto Jesus	203
	Endnotes	215

Dedication

To our sons:
Calvin Lewis and Justin Lewis

"The father of a righteous man has great joy; he who has a wise son delights in him. May your father and mother be glad; may she who gave you birth rejoice!"

(Prov. 23: 24,25).

Foreword

This book has two titles: *God's Hall of Fame* and the *Trials and Triumph of Faith* – and if you can't see yourself in the first you can surely see yourself in the second!

This reminds us that the roll-call of honour in Hebrews chapter eleven is not an exercise in elitism, though some of these names are truly illustrious. To change the metaphor, it is not only a series of paintings of the high and mighty in the history of redemption but also a series of mirrors in which we may see ourselves in stirring possibilities.

Here we learn that we have, each of us, our place and part in the *continuing* story of God's people. Our name is in the index and our life of faith has its paragraph. As we look back to Abraham or Moses or Deborah or David we are reading about *our* spiritual ancestors too (Rom. 4:16,17)

When we read scripture we are reading *our* story as well as theirs. These are our people, this is our story, this is our song.

Moreover, Peter tells us that their story will not be complete without ours (2 Pet. 1:12) and the writer to the Hebrews has them seated in the arena of faith cheering us on as we run the race marked out for us (Heb. 12:1).

Whatever the trials of faith, its triumphs are sure because *Jesus* has gone before us: deeper than any of us in suffering, higher than any of us in glory and joy, the pioneer and perfecter of our faith 'who, for the joy that was set before him, endured the cross' (Heb. 12.2).

With Jesus before us we can journey on as confident as any prophet, as glad as any psalmist, for 'we have the word of the prophets made more certain, and you would do well to pay attention to it, as to the light shining in a dark place, until the day dawns and the morning star rises in your hearts' (2 Pet. 1:19).

As usual, I am bound to record with much gratitude and

appreciation the work of Mrs. Barbara Walters in typing this and others of my books, the appreciation and encouragement of the Cornerstone Church elders and members whom I am privileged to serve, and the unfailing love, wisdom and support of Valerie, 'the elect lady' whom I love.

Peter Lewis,
The Cornerstone Evangelical Church,
Nottingham

1

CELEBRATION OF FAITH

Genes and Jesus

Three thousand years ago, the Psalmist sang 'I praise you because I am fearfully and wonderfully made' (Ps 139:14). Just how wonderfully we are made, at one level at least, is currently being uncovered by modern genetic research. The human genome project currently under way will, by its conclusion in 2005, know the order of the three billion letters that constitute our genetic make-up.[1]

How much of the human being is determined and defined by their genes is a much bigger and more difficult issue, one involving human psychology, human spirituality and, above all, God our Creator. Some scientists see it differently. Recently Professor Francis Crick, who discovered the structure of DNA, suggested perhaps half-seriously, that there may be a religious gene, one that determines whether an individual becomes a believer. In an interview in *The Times* he wondered out loud if there might be something in people's brains which made them more susceptible to religion than others and whether if was inherited or not or produced by early training.[2]

Now when, as Christian believers, we are faced with a mixture of scientific knowledge and personal speculation it is important not to write off the whole thing but to recognise scientific facts as God-made realities and to separate out the presuppositions (eg that science is all) and to compare the scientific facts with the claims of Christianity.

It is widely accepted that there are elements in our individual physical and psychological make-up which predispose us in various ways. For instance, some people might be more prone to addictions than others, some may have an unusually strong sexual drive and some may have

1

a more philosophical or mystical bent and thus may be more inclined to religious interests and patterns of behaviour than others. However, Christianity is not the same as a religious sense, nor is it simply the study of religious experience. Christianity is based on concrete historical facts, on an historic person and a call which is addressed to all kinds of persons at all times and in all places. Jesus did not say, 'Come unto me all you who are genetically inclined,' but, 'Come unto me all you who are weary and burdened and I will give you rest' (Mt 11:28). The gospel of Jesus is not for a 'type' of person but for all types of sinners who all need the Saviour, and faith is the gift of God which is given to all kinds of people, the practically minded as well as the mystically inclined.

A few days after the interview with Francis Crick appeared, I was delighted to read in the 'Letters' page of *The Times* a wise and characteristically witty response from an old college friend, the Reverend Brian Maiden of Heaton Moor, Stockport. It read:

> Sir, Presumably some people, like Francis Crick, possess a gene which predisposes them to be 'scientific'. This tells us nothing about the truth or falsity of scientific theories, which are based (with some exceptions) on empirical evidence.
>
> Such theories, when demonstrated to be true, are equally true for everyone, even for those whose genetic make-up does not incline them to be interested in such things.
>
> In this respect science is similar to Christianity, which is based on factual, historical events (Lk 1:1–4 etc) and is therefore true regardless of our genetic make up. For this reason it may be particularly attractive for those of us who lack a religious gene and possess a scientific one, as well as for those who possess both.[3]

Revelation and celebration

The Bible nowhere gives a formal definition of faith. The nearest statement we have to that is at the beginning of

Hebrews chapter 11. However, even here, we have not so much a definition of faith as 'a recommendation and celebration' of faith followed by a demonstration of faith at work in human lives responding to God's call, enduring through all discouragements and gaining what was promised.

The religion of the Bible is emphatically a religion of *revelation* not of intuition or of speculation. The initiative of God, the living God, the personal God, the *speaking* God, is everywhere foremost in Old Testament and in New. By his Spirit his life-bringing, light-bearing word creates faith in the human heart and it is in response to this that faith comes into its own. As Jesus said: 'The Spirit give life; the flesh counts for nothing. The words I have spoken to you are spirit and they are life' (Jn 6:63)

For faith God's word is decisive, his promise is the substantial ground on which it builds, and his promises about the future are allowed to shape and guide us in the present. As one scholar, Kaseman, puts it: 'Faith arises when a person lets himself be convinced by God and so attains a certainty which is objectively grounded and which transcends all human possibilities in its reliability.'[4]

Biblical faith is always a response to revelation. It is therefore not a leap in the dark but a step into the light. It is not a vague mysticism but an understanding response to a clearly revealed truth. True faith is not blind but on the contrary cries out, 'I was blind but now I see.' It is a joyful response to God's initiative and in-breaking to a life. *In all ages faith has had this supreme characteristic: it recognises and responds to God's revelation of himself.* Jesus put it most simply and memorably when he said: 'My sheep listen to my voice; I know them and they follow me. I give them eternal life and they shall never perish; no one can snatch them out of my hand' (Jn 10:27). This is faith's foundation, faith's confidence and faith's security; it is also faith's joy – a joy celebrated in the first lines of Hebrews chapter 11.

Before he comes to the various examples of faith, the writer of Hebrews speaks of faith itself in memorable and famous words. Those words, as we shall see, are not as well rendered in the New International Version as in the older Authorised Version and we shall begin our study with some biblical and theological thinking about faith before we come on to the practical examples that follow.

Faith with substance

'Now faith is being sure of what we hope for and certain of what we do not see' (Heb 11:1, NIV).

'Now faith is the substance of things hoped for, the evidence of things not seen' (Heb 11:1, AV).

There are many things we know but can't easily explain. We can say of so much, as Augustine said of time, 'I know well enough what it is provided that nobody asks me; but if I am asked what it is and try to explain, I am baffled'! It is hard, too, for Christians to explain their faith or define it in an abstract and formal way. This is not surprising, for the content of faith is its object and faith exists to point to that object and not to itself. We cannot easily speak of our faith in the abstract for we cannot abstract it from the One in whom we have faith. Faith explains that which is believed rather than itself in believing; its confidence and security does not lie in itself but in that which it rests on. Faith lives, not striving to will something into existence but resting on something God has brought into existence.

The writer to the Hebrews knows this and defines faith here in strikingly objective ways. He actually says, not that faith is the 'assurance' of things hoped for (as NIV) but that faith is the *substance* (Greek *hypostasis*) of things hoped for. He uses a Greek word which designates an objective reality in contrast to mere appearance. He is not speaking of faith as merely a subjective feeling but of its existence in a person as being itself an objective guarantee, a sort of title deed to the future of God, a reality and a gift from God which gets its substance from the certainties which lie ahead for us but which are already present in God.

Faith can grasp the future in the present as a substantial

4

reality because the future already exists in God in principle and in embryo. God does not dwell in the future; the future dwells in God. His promise reveals its embryonic existence; his Kingdom begins its present life in the world; his on-going activity will complete and fulfil its existence. Faith hears the word, lays hold of the promise and acts accordingly. Hence faith lives in the light and power of the future even in the present and is thus the substance of things hoped for.

The writer of Hebrews goes on to say that faith is 'the "evidence" (Greek *elenchos*) of what we do not (yet) see'. Again he uses a word which means more than the feeling of certainty; he uses a word which here means 'proof', 'evidence', 'demonstration'. His point is that faith lays hold on the word of God and thereby becomes the demonstration of things not seen. It brings the future into the present in unique ways; it counteracts and even overcomes present realities with future realities. Where God has put true faith he has given a piece of the future in the present, a personal experience of what is yet to come and what cannot be known by sight or touch or any physical sense but what is sure and certain in God.

Faith with a future

We learn from this that biblical faith is focused not so much on the invisible in contrast to the visible as the future in contrast to the present. William Lane, in his learned commentary on Hebrews, comments on the reference in our verse to what is not seen:

> The contrast implied in the phrase is thus not between the visible phenomenal world of sense perception below and the invisible, heavenly world of reality above, as in Platonism, but between events already witnessed as part of the historic past and events as yet unseen because they belong to the eschatological future.[5]

5

The forward-looking character of faith is demonstrated throughout this chapter in the lives of the Old Testament heroes that follow. It is to be demonstrated, too, in our own lives in the 'real' world – for nothing is more real than the approaching future and the realities which Jesus Christ will bring with him at his Second Coming.

Faith with a past

We too may be certain of what we do not yet see because the same Christ who has undoubtedly come has said that he will undoubtedly come again. Jesus unites in himself the past, present and future focus of faith. Because of him, faith is not a leap in the dark but a reasonable trust. It is a response to something which was done in the public realm. Into our world, in space and time, Someone came who didn't fit any of our categories. He was clearly a man; yet he said he was the Son of God whom the Father had sent into the world. He was born in Bethlehem and raised as a boy in Nazareth; yet he said he had had glory with the Father before the world was. As a good Jew he was a descendant of Abraham; yet he said, 'Before Abraham was, I am.' He stood in the line of the prophets yet he said things no prophet would have dared to say. He said that the prophets had spoken to him and that history had led up to him and a new history would proceed from him. He claimed that he was the world's hope and Saviour. He called all men and women to believe him, to come to him and to commit themselves fully to him.

Now we have all these things in solid history. They are the solid basis of trust. If you can trust Jesus you can trust him about the future, about heaven, about salvation and the new world which will come with him. This, with the knowledge of his atoning death and glorious resurrection, attested by many witnesses, themselves reasonable, trustworthy men and women, gives us a basis for faith as reasonable trust. The historic Jesus is the basis of faith.

The Spirit of faith

However, true faith is never simply an assent to what lies in history, past or future. It also involves a personal commitment to the living and coming-again Christ as Saviour and Lord. Faith is not simply consent to a creed but commitment to a Person. Here the work of the Holy Spirit is crucial, for by nature we are very unwilling to let God be God in our lives: sin has darkened our minds with respect to the truth about God and hardened our hearts so that we can remain unmoved by the gospel of Jesus Christ and unwilling to let go our self-centredness, to recognise our sinfulness and to come to him in repentance and faith and self-giving.

When the Holy Spirit comes with saving power into our lives he enlightens our minds so that we begin to understand as we never understood before; he touches and warms emotions long cold towards the love of God so that we are moved and convicted by the death of Jesus for us; he works in our wills with all the persuasive love of God communicating a strong and joyful power so that we willingly kneel in repentance and determined self-giving to the God who gave us so much and to the Christ who died so willingly that we might live. The Holy Spirit is the mainspring of the greatest change in our lives: faith is his gift, new life his power and sheer undeserved love his motivation. As John Calvin beautifully puts it: 'Faith is the proper and entire work of the Holy Spirit, illumined by whom we recognise God and the treasures of his kindness.'[6]

The great Reformer's teaching on faith is full of a sense of its God-given power and beauty. The Holy Spirit is the bond by which Christ effectively unites us to himself. He inspires in us that faith which receives the good of what Christ has done for us. Faith is the principle work of the Holy Spirit, and the faith which he inspires, even though it often has to wrestle with doubts, has at its heart and kernel a confident reliance on God's love:

Now we shall possess a right definition of faith if we call it a firm and certain knowledge of God's benevolence toward us, founded upon the truth of the freely given promise in Christ, both revealed in our minds and sealed upon our hearts through the Holy Spirit.[7]

Enduring hope

It is this faith which in turn produces biblical hope: 'Faith is the substance of things hoped for.' In our use of the word today, hope is often a synonym for uncertainty (as when we hope for good weather on our holidays!). In the Bible however, hope is nearer to expectation: it is a strong and patient attitude which awaits a promised result. God is the source and basis of hope (Jer 17:7, 13) and so hope is not uncertain. Correspondingly, Hebrews tells us that hope in the glorified Christ is an anchor that grips an immovable throne (Heb 6:19). The New Testament focuses the hope of believers on the Second Coming of Christ when 'Christ Jesus our hope' (1 Tim 1:1) will come to a waiting and faithful Church: 'We wait for the blessed hope – the glorious appearing of our great God and Saviour, Jesus Christ' (Titus 2:13). Meantime it gives a call to patient endurance through many trials and here offers us a series of great examples of faith and hope. Here there are many things we do not understand, many disappointed hopes, many trials and temptations which threaten to loosen our grip on Christ. It is only as we 'fix our eyes on Jesus' (Heb 12:2) that we can survive the doubts and surmount the problems. In the celebrated words of Anselm: 'I do not seek to understand that I may believe, but I believe that I may understand: for this I also believe, that unless I believe I will not understand.'

In the Cathedral in Copenhagen, Denmark, there are along the walls, life-sized statues of the Apostles. At the front is the magnificent Thorwolden statue of Christ. However, while the faces of the other figures can be easily seen, it is said you will not be able to look full into the face of the Christ figure unless you kneel at its feet. That is where faith grows strong and hope endures: at the feet of Jesus, the Saviour of the world.

2

FAITH RECOGNISING ITS CREATOR

'By faith we understand that the universe was formed at God's command' (Heb 11:3).

The phenomenal sales of Stephen Hawkings' book *A Brief History of Time* (10 million hardback copies world-wide) show our concern with *roots*. We all want to know where we came from, how it all began and how we came to be here. However, comparatively few who possess the book can understand it fully. Indeed, Richard Feynmann, said to be the greatest theoretical physicist of modern times used to say that *no one* understood quantum mechanics! Like an unread Bible on a bookshelf, Hawk-ings' book is, I suspect, for many a talisman in which they have blind faith – only one which puts God on the dubious margins rather than in the emphatic centre.

Understanding creation

A Dutch professor of science in the Technical University of Delft, A. van den Beukel, who is a Christian, protests strongly at the famous closing words of Stephen Hawk-ings' book. The book ends confident in the physicists' ability to discover 'a complete theory of the universe' understandable by everyone, and concludes: 'Then we shall all, philosophers, scientists and just ordinary people, be able to take part in the discussion of the question of why it is that we and the universe exist.'

The boundless arrogance [van den Beukel protests]. Throughout their long history, human beings have yet to say a meaningful word on the question 'Why do we

11

and the universe exist?' This discussion can only begin when the scientists have finished. Then the Great Formula will be explained to human beings and even simple souls will be enlightened. Then they may take part in the discussion.[1]

A pity, he goes on to say, about Jesus Christ who it seems was born about two thousand years too early to take part in it – not to mention thinkers of every age and ordinary people who foolishly thought they could 'understand' before physics came into its own.

The writer of Hebrews, however, dares to say we *can* understand our context in creation in one supreme and vital respect: 'By faith we understand that the universe was formed at God's command.' Such an understanding is not simply the result of faith as a natural intuition (though we all have that too, Rom 1:18–19), but of faith as a believing response to revelation. He is clearly referring back to the opening chapter of the Bible and to the repeated refrain in Genesis 1: 'And God said, "Let there be..." and there was...' In Genesis 1 we read: 'In the beginning God created the heavens and the earth' and it becomes clear that he did so by a creating, commanding and ordering word which had 'performative power in calling forth and ordering the visible universe'. His point is that faith reads (or hears) this revelation and receives it as true in awe and gratitude and so understands that *the secret of the universe is not a formula but a Person*. The first concern of Genesis 1 is not the *how* but the *who* of creation. It is our privilege to ransack creation for its secrets; we were made to enquire, to search, to find out, but we were made first and foremost to know God who made us and our world, and we fail deeply if we fail to understand him.

Understanding ourselves

In his book *Understanding the Present: Science and the Soul of man* Bryan Appleyard writes in passionate protest not against science rightly used but against *scientism* – the belief that science is the complete and only explanation of the universe and that scientists alone hold the the key to the meaning, purpose and justification of human life:

> We are in possession of an unprecedently effective way of understanding and acting called science. We have seen that this way is intolerent, restless and ambitious, that it supplants religion and culture, yet does not answer the needs once answered by religion and cultures.[2]

'Science', he warns, 'quietly and inexplicitly, is talking us into abandoning ourselves, our true selves'.[3] As it holds back from the moral or transcendent, so scientfic liberalism also holds back from providing the individual with an awareness of his place in the world. 'On the maps provided by science we find everything except ourselves'. [4] At the end of his lengthy investigation Appleyard concludes:

> Science begins by saying it can answer only *this* kind of question and ends by claiming that *these* are the only questions that can be asked. Once the implications and shallowness of this trick are fully realised, science will be humbled and we shall be free to celebrate ourselves again.[5]

To discover that you are the child of a heavenly Father and not just the product of impersonal forces, to discover that there is a Face behind the stars and that you are not lost in the vast universe but known and named and loved is the greatest of life's discoveries and our supreme comfort in life's distress. The suffering Christian Jews of Hebrews needed to know that their's was a God:

> Whose love is as great as his power
> And knows neither measure nor end.[6]

13

And in our modern world we need to know it too.

Understanding our place

It is a tragic mistake to measure the size of the universe over against the size of a human being and then proclaim (however sadly) that the human being is irrelevant in cosmic terms. Imagine you are looking from a vantage point on a great mountain towering above the landscape. Suddenly you notice lines of vehicles converging at its foot and another line of climbers aiming for a dot on a cliff face. That dot is, in terms of size, irrelevant to the mountain; but who thinks that is any factor in determining the value of the person trapped on the cliff helpless and hurt but so valuable as to command widespread concern and all the resources of modern technology? So science alone cannot value us; it can, however, help us when valued. Its place is in subservience to our humanity and our knowledge of our own self-worth. We are made to know our world and its setting; we are made to know our place in the cosmos and our place there is not unimportant. The baby weighs more than the mountain; the stargazer more than the stars!

'Lost in wonder...'

We still look up in awe; we too look around in wonder; we see not only the frighteningly vast size and scale of the universe, but the fascinating and beautiful order into which God has brought the complex forces of creation in our own world – and as we look we wonder and speculate and hope. A short while ago, my wife (who was trained as a painter) took me to The Tate in St Ives during a holiday in Cornwall. Among the paintings was one by John Wells (1907) entitled *Painting Aspiring Forms* (1950). I found it pleasing enough as a painting but was even more attracted by the words on the card placed alongside it. Wells wrote to a friend the following description of his feeling about

14

making abstract art. It is itself a beautiful word-picture of the artist's wonder at the world around him:

> The morning air and the sea's blue light with points of diamond and the gorse incandescent beyond the trees; countless rocks ragged or round and of every colour; birds resting or flying, and the sense of a multitude of creatures living out their minute lives all this is part of one's life and I want desperately to express it; not just what I see but what I feel about it ... But how can one paint the warmth of the sun, the sound of the sea, the journey of a beetle across a rock, or thoughts of one's own whence and whither?

The painter sees it and wants to capture it in paint, this wondrous creation; the poet wants to put it in words, the musician in sounds. But it is not difficult to detect a note of frustration, of unsatisfied yearning, of unsure hope in so much that is expressed. We were made to worship – but not to worship an 'unknown God' (Acts 17:23).

'... love and praise'

We were made to wonder at creation around us – but not to be deaf to the creator who explains his world as his own and himself as holy. We were made above all to be worshippers who hear God's word in his Word and who thus understand that 'the universe was formed at God's command': 'The heavens declare the glory of God; the skies proclaim the work of his hands. Day after day they pour forth speech; night after night they display knowledge' (Ps 19:1–2). 'O Lord, our Lord, how majestic is your name in all the earth! You have set your glory above the heavens. From the lips of children and infants you have ordained praise' (Ps 8:1–2).

The rest of the Bible unfolds in continuity with this. God is not just left 'up there' as the prime mover; he speaks and shows himself as the one who has made us 'in his image' and for obedient, loving, worshipful fellowship with him. He is the God who stays even when we rebel and fill our world with violence and exploitation. He is the one who continues to speak, who sends his prophets and finally his Son. He is never the absentee landlord but the caring, suffering, judging and saving God. It is by his ongoing work in the world that we understand his initial work in the world; it is as we know him as Saviour that we most fully know him as creator.

A redeemed creation

Scripture unfolds this purpose in God: that he who *created* the world will *redeem* it. He will redeem the very planet as well as the race that inherited it and spoiled it. Human sin brought upon the whole creation and its environment a curse (Gen 3:17–19). In the words of the Apostle Paul: 'The creation was subjected to frustration'. Because of human sin 'the whole creation has been groaning' ever since (Rom 8:20–2). Moreover, throughout our human history we have abused our environment and misused our trust from God. In a careful and scholarly study of this, Thomas Derr writes:

> Over-grazing, deforestation and similar errors of sufficient magnitude to destroy civilisations, have been committed by Egyptians, Romans, North Africans, Persians, Indians, Aztecs and Buddhists (as well as 'Christians'). Centuries before the Christian era Plato commented, in his *Critias*, on the deforestation of Attica. Since primitive times man has been altering his environment dramatically in ways that upset the ecological balances. Early hunters used fire to drive out their game. Agricultural people everywhere clear fields and dam streams and wipe out stock predators and kill plants that get in the way of their chosen crops.[7]

The fall of man has affected the whole ecosystem in various and profound ways. Yet the time will come when 'the creation itself will be liberated from its bondage to decay and brought into the glorious freedom of the children of God' (Rom 8:21). As the physical creation shared in the consequences of our fall, so it will share in the consequences of our redemption. The basis and guarantee of this is the atoning and reconciling work of Christ. The Son of God 'by whom all things were created' and in whom 'all things hold together' has reconciled a fallen creation, as well as a fallen race, to God: 'For God was pleased to have all his fullness dwell in him and through him to reconcile to himself all things, whether things on earth or things in heaven, by making peace through his blood, shed on the cross' (Col 1:19–20). That is why the New Testament ends with 'a new heaven and a new earth' (Rev 21:1); a renewal of the cosmos by the power of Christ at his Second Coming. The Bible not only has a theology of creation but a Christology of creation.

This is the basis of a Christian understanding of *ecology*, a subject widely seen as of very great importance in our modern world which threatens to destroy itself by its own progress! We must have progress – no one should want to turn back the clock – but it should be progress with a responsibility to ourselves as a race and to our world as stewards entrusted with its development and its good (Gen 1:28;2:15). Christians are to live lives which anticipate earth's final destiny. Every time we pray, 'Your kingdom come,' we look forward to the new world but in its beginnings the kingdom has already come with the Lord Jesus Christ and we are, even now, a part of it. We have been touched with its power and healing. We live in its light and its vision and in the expectation of its final coming in fullness. We are already the people of the kingdom, living by its standards and practising its principles.

Among those principles is our regard for God's creation and our own preparation for the day of its renewal by beginning in some small way the process of recovery and restoration now – in our homes, towns and cities, in our gardens and our countryside, in our decreasing forests and our expanding deserts, in developed and under-developed

17

countries. So we should meet pollution with protest, wastage with economy, neglect with care, exploitation with conservation, ignorance with understanding. It is Christians who should be most truly friends of the earth because we are friends of God who made it and of Christ who will redeem it.

3

FAITH RESENTED
AND HONOURED (ABEL)

'*By faith Abel offered God a better sacrifice than Cain did.
By faith he was commended as a righteous man, when God
spoke well of his offerings. And by faith he still speaks
even though he is dead*' (Heb 11:4).

Some of the most powerful forces of life are invisible and
seen only by their effects. We cannot see the wind but we
can see the tree-tops moving furiously as they are buffeted.
We cannot see electricity but we respect its presence and
its potency as we switch on a light or an electric fire. We
cannot see love but we can know its presence by its effects
such as commitment, tenderness and help.

And so it is with faith. We know it by what it does, for
though in point of our acceptance by God, faith and works
are to be strictly kept apart (Rom 3:20,28;5:1) yet in point
of our consequent life with God, faith and works are to
be constantly kept together (Jas 2:14–26). Good works
are not the basis of our new life with God but they are
the fruit and demonstration of our new life with God.
They indicate and reveal the presence of true faith.

From now on we are going to have a series of practical
demonstrations rather than theological definitions of faith.
For in the verses that follow, faith is defined by what it
does, it is seen in its effects and we shall see the strength
and beauty of faith and, I hope, the attraction of the life
of faith.

Children of the eighth day

Here are two brothers. They have the same parents, the
same background, the same difficulties and the same

19

encouragements. I refer to difficulties because they have both grown up under the shadow of a great loss. Their parents had first known life in a situation of great privilege: in the Garden of Eden, in a condition of sinless happiness and plenty and enjoying an unspoiled intimacy with God. They had fallen, disobeyed and rebelled against him, seduced by the serpent, Satan, into thinking they too could be as God. The result was exile from the Garden into a world of hardships, a world cursed by sin. Worse, death entered the race which had been made for eternal life and a process was begun which was to involve their children and all their descendants in a history of rebellion and corruption. Yet, here is something wonderful: God did not leave them, though sin hid him from them in many ways. God went out with them into a spoiled world and began the long process of gathering to himself in salvation sinful men and women, rescuing fallen humanity, touching hearts with contrition and hope, repentance and faith.

Cain and Abel were 'children of the eighth day', as one writer puts it.[1] The perfect goodness of the six-day creation had been corrupted by their parents, Adam and Eve. Futility had entered the world and humanity was now a flawed image of its creator. True religion had not died out in the world but false religion was alive and well, and in this story we meet both.

> Now Abel kept flocks, and Cain worked the soil. In the course of time Cain brought some of the fruits of the soil as an offering to the Lord. But Abel brought fat portions from some of the firstborn of his flock. The Lord looked with favour on Abel and his offering, but on Cain and his offering he did not look with favour. So Cain was very angry, and his face was downcast (Gen 4:2b–5).

Worship acceptable and unacceptable

Some have thought that Cain's sacrifice was rejected because it was bloodless. This is unlikely since even later, in the Levitical laws, grain offerings are quite acceptable. Not all sacrifices were of the same kind. Other commentators have detected a difference between the two brothers in their approach to worship, since Abel offered the choicest animals from his flock while Cain merely offered 'some produce of the land'. This may be the case, revealing an attitude of faith and love in Abel which is absent in Cain, and which says, like David, 'I will not sacrifice to the Lord my God burnt offerings that cost me nothing' (2 Sam 24:24).

What is clear from a number of Scriptures is that the great reason for the acceptance of one offering and the rejection of another lay not in the offering but in the person bringing the offering. Hebrews 11:5 touches the fundamental difference: 'By faith Abel offered God a better sacrifice than Cain did.' However, the writer immediately links faith to life as do all the other writers who mention him: 'By faith he was commended as a righteous man.' Similarly, other biblical references to Cain make it clear that the difference between the brothers and the reason for God's acceptance of the one and his rejection of the other involved their very different characters and conduct. Cain was altogether an unregenerate man and his life showed it.

However, even unregenerate people like to worship sometimes – and can be fiercely indignant if any doubt is cast on the acceptableness of their worship. They forget a fundamental truth about all true worship: that the giver is not acceptable because of the gift; the gift is acceptable because of the giver. Calvin says of Abel: 'His sacrifice pleased God because he himself was pleasing to God.' If the worshipper is not in a right relationship with God, the worship can never be acceptable to God. The God of truth calls for sincerity of heart. Cain's double-standard revealed his insincerity. God says to Cain: 'If you do what is right will you not be accepted? But if you do not do what is right, sin is crouching at your door; it desires to have you, but you must master it' (Gen 4:6–7). The Apostle John writes: 'Do not be like Cain, who belonged to the evil one and murdered his brother. And why did he murder him? Because his own actions were evil and his brother's were righteous' (1 Jn 3:12).

In the event God's warnings were not heeded and his invitation was refused. The wild beast at the door was not resisted; it sprang and Cain was taken over by it. It did not have to be like that but it was. In the end it was not the presence of sin but the absence of faith which was decisive and final for Cain as it is for anyone who is deaf to the voice of God calling them to repentance and faith.

Offensive worship

Cain's sacrifice had been rejected because of an unseen, but real, state of heart and corresponding actions in his life. Cain's life was offensive and inevitably his worship was offensive to God. It is a great mistake to imagine that worship can make up for life; that words alone can please God or liturgy or beautiful music skilfully played or fine singing which does not proceed from a sincere heart. If your life is false, your worship can never be true. The writer to the Hebrews will tell us that 'without faith it is impossible to please God' (Heb 11:6) and no one can claim to have true faith if their life is false and their religion an outward show. True faith is an active thing, a working principle within, which challenges us, guides us, encourages us and leads us on to good works (Jas 2:18).

The Apostle Paul, writing to the Romans, urges his readers 'in view of God's mercy' to offer their bodies 'as living sacrifices, holy and pleasing to God' and asserts 'this is your spiritual [Greek *logike*, reasonable] act of worship' (Rom 12:1). In speaking like this he teaches us that unless our lives are consistent our worship can never be logical, we cannot sin with our bodies and sing with our souls. The prophet Isaiah, long before Paul, warned that worship itself can be an insult to God (Is 1:10–17) if it is false. Cain's offering was not a gift but a bribe. He did not come in humility but in arrogance as his anger shows. He did not come in humble faith but in the spirit of a transaction; my offering to make up my sin. Such bargains can never be struck with the true God who is holy and uncompromising (Mic 6:6–8). 'He has showed you, O man, what is good. And what does the Lord require of you? To act justly and to love mercy and to walk humbly with your God' (Mic 6:8).

When false religion meets true

Cain is the mirror image of his brother, 'righteous Abel' (Mt 23:35). Abel too is a child of the eighth day, a sinner struggling with the hard realities of life. But he brings to God his best not as a bribe but as a thank-offering, not to gain credit but to show gratitude, not to counter-balance sin but to seek God. With Abel the act of worship was the first-fruits of a life given to God; with Cain it was all there was, and so when God accepted his brother's offering and rejected his own, Cain's anger burned first against God and then against his brother: 'And while they were in the field, Cain attacked his brother Abel and killed him' (Gen 4:8). Those destitute of true faith have never understood those rich in it. Those without faith not only do not understand those who have it, they often actively resent it, especially when they themselves are somewhat religious. Men and women of faith are often most resented by those who have an alternative faith, one which is undemanding, unchallenging and without the power to change a life. When false religion meets true, when its self-image is disturbed, its authenticity questioned, its fraud exposed – then resentment bursts into flame and the anger of Cain burns in a new situation.

God loves you

Sometimes, of course, Cain is more impressive than Abel in life. It is important to say this because many true believers (perhaps you among them!) struggle with great temptations, some find themselves in the grip of terrible circumstances, some emerge from dreadful backgrounds with scarred spirits and damaged emotions. They may not in some respects bear much comparison with the balanced personality and character of their unbelieving neighbour or colleague who had it easy from the cradle. They may even envy their talents or personality or control and ability to cope.

Yet there may be this crucial difference between them: one has faith in the struggles and the failures and another has none and sees no need of it. We shall see this illustrated in a later story with two other brothers. For all I know, Esau may have been a better character than Jacob in many ways, but Jacob had faith: he wrestled with God for the blessing – and he got it! Hebrews 11:4 makes it clear that it really was faith that made the critical difference between Cain and Abel too.

And you: you may regret many things deeply about your past; you may in some things hate yourself; but you have learned that God loves you, that Christ died for you and that God hasn't finished with you yet. You are Abel not Cain, a child of God not of the devil. For all your failures you can say like Peter after he denied his Lord: 'Lord you know all things; you *know* that I love you (Jn 21:17). You have faith and your faith pleases God; it delights him because it is his gift and he sees what you shall one day be. In his justice of course, God could have rejected both Abel and Cain – for Abel too was a sinner. But in his freedom God chose Abel, gave him his gift of faith and fostered his spirit of righteousness and love; just as later he would choose younger Jacob over older Esau (Gen 25:21–3) and just as he would choose Israel among the nations (Deut 7:6–7). Here are deep lessons in sovereignty and grace, and here too we have something which we see both in history and in our own experience.

God can use you

Moreover, as God has chosen you so God can use you; he can use your testimony, your struggles, your life of faith and your sacrifice of praise in your own family, among fellow-workers and friends. He can reach others with your hope who see your faith and its effects. We read of Abel: 'And by faith he still speaks even though he is dead' (Heb 11:4). It may be after your death that your faith becomes a legacy for your children or grandchildren. You never know the full extent and impact of your witness as a believing Christian person. You may feel it has been rejected yet God may use it still, even years later. None of us can measure the potential of a life of faith and only the Last Day will reveal all it has achieved.

There is a memorable story which illustrates this, told of one of the old English Puritan preachers, the Reverend John Flavel. Towards the end of the seventeenth century, Flavel was preaching to his congregation in Dartmouth from Paul's words: 'If any man love not the Lord Jesus let him be *anathema* (i.e. accursed), *maranatha* (i.e. our Lord is coming)' (1 Cor 16:22AV). At the end he rose to pronounce the benediction but found himself unable to do so. Instead, the old preacher said with much feeling, 'How shall I bless this assembly, when every person in it who does not love the Lord is anathema, maranatha'? His words had such a powerful effect that the entire congregation was deeply affected. One, a member of the gentry, 'fell to the floor senseless'.

In the congregation was a fifteen-year-old boy, Luke Short. Soon after, the boy went to sea and sailed to America where he became a farmer. There he lived a long and healthy life and even at a hundred years of age he still worked on his farm. One day out in a field he began to look back on his life. He remembered the scene which had taken place eighty-five years before and the old preacher's words at the end came back to him with great force. Deeply convicted of sin and especially his failure to seek God for salvation despite his opportunities in youth, Luke Short there and then fell to his knees in the field, repented, and believed in the Lord Jesus. He joined the congregational church in his town, Middlesborough, and lived on, a true Christian until his death at a hundred and sixteen years of age!

It is not only Abel whose faith speaks, even though he is dead. Your faith, your prayers, your words and deeds of testimony to God can carry a message down the years in the memory of those who have known you so that it can be said of you, 'And by faith they still speak even though they are dead.'

4

FAITH WALKING WITH GOD (ENOCH)

'By faith Enoch was taken from this life, so that he did not experience death; he could not be found, because God had taken him away. For before he was taken, he was commended as one who pleased God' (Heb 11:5).

Who are the truly great people in life? Our thoughts might fly at first to the men and women of great achievement, wealth, skill, talent, beauty. But my question is not what are the truly great things people have done, but who are the truly great *people* in life. Our achievements, talents etc. are one thing but *we* are another. A great musician, politician, sportsman or woman, or entertainer may not be a great human being, may even be a deeply-flawed, spoiled, failed human being. Public success may hide private failure; public applause may mock family pain. I do not mean there is no greatness in human talents and fine achievements or in the people who achieve them. Far from it. But the kind of greatness I am concerned with here is in the person as a person and apart from their gifts or achievements; it is a greatness that would remain if the gift were lost and it is a greatness that very 'ordinary' people in life can and do possess.

In his book *God in the Wasteland*, David Wells makes an interesting observation:

At the beginning of the nineteenth century, most obituaries made some mention of the character of the deceased; by the end of the century this was rarely the case. By contrast a person's occupation was seldom an important detail in obituaries at the beginning of the nineteenth century but by 1990 it had become the key means by which a person was identified. This substitution of function for character is consistent both with the use of anonymity in our large, complex and specialised world and with a new sense that it is inappropriate to define a person on the basis of character in a public context that offers no consensus concerning (and if it comes to that is not much interested in) what constitutes good character.[1]

If we have any developed moral sense we shall go through life looking for character as well as cleverness, for integrity as well as achievement and valuing the virtues above the talents. However, this passage leads us higher still and commends neither the life of talent nor even the life of virtue but the life of *faith*.

The man who walked with God

We know little about Enoch and he is commended for one thing only. In the Genesis record he is not named with the 'big' men of Genesis 4. He is not a builder of cities or a leader of warriors; he is not the forger of tools or the father of nomadic tribes with their flocks and herds; he is not even skilful with music and the arts. He is known for one thing: 'Enoch walked with God; then he was no more for God took him away' (Gen 5: 24).

In the ancient geneology of Genesis chapter 5 we have those ancient names and baffling ages, but after each name and immense tale of years we have the repeated refrain like a drumbeat in a funeral march – 'and then he died . . . and then he died . . . and then he died'. When we come to Enoch, however, the refrain is suspended and a new note is sounded clear and sweet: 'Enoch walked with God; then he was no more, because God took him away' (Gen 5:24). The meaning is clear, but the writer to the Hebrews is specific: 'he did not experience death' (Heb 11:5).

This is often called the 'translation' of Enoch (his translation from earth to heaven) and in the Old Testament it is only matched by the translation of Elijah the prophet who was taken to heaven in a whirlwind (2 Kgs 2:11). However, it is not Enoch's miraculous exit *from* the world which is our writer's great concern so much as his faithful life *in* the

28

world: 'For before he was taken he was commended as one who pleased God' (Heb 11:5). In our Old Testament version we read in Genesis; 'Enoch walked with God', but in the ancient Greek version of the Hebrew Old Testament, the Septuagint, it was translated 'Enoch pleased God' and that is the version our writer quotes here. It does not matter about the different expression used; they mean the same thing. Enoch pleased God by believing in him, coming to him, walking with him in faith: the faith that works by love. And Enoch did so knowing that the supreme thing was not worldly success but a heavenly inheritance.

Our walk with God

It may have been no easy thing for Enoch to walk with God in a world ripening fast for judgement and the Flood. There has never, in fact, been a time in our fallen world when it was easy to walk with God. It is not easy now, but Enoch's God is as alive and as good and can be as close to us as he was to Enoch and we too can live as Enoch did and walk in the real world with the real God.

There is an aquatic species of spider which, though air-breathing, lives on the mud at the bottom of ponds. It survives under water by going at intervals to the surface and trapping oxygen in a bubble between the hairs on its body. Then it descends to the bottom of the pond, able to breath under water. We too, as believers, live in a world whose atmosphere is often inimical to our faith. We have to survive spiritually in an alien element and can only do so if we take from a regular prayer-life and reading of God's word our spiritual oxygen into that element with us.

A walk with God has its own atmosphere and brings its own strength and perspective into a world which has never made a life of faith easy for the believer.

Lonely places

If you walk with God you will often walk *in lonely places.* Jesus said that 'only a few' found the small gate and narrow road that lead to life (Mt 7:14). Only a few find it because most do not care to look for it or recognise it when it stands in front of them. They prefer a wide gate and a broad road heedless that it 'leads to destruction'. They prefer their image of God to the Son who *is* his image and hence are deaf to his words that he is the gate (Jn 10:7, 9) and the only way to God (Jn 14:6). Jesus calls, but so do other voices offering heaven on easier terms and a life 'uncramped' by the restrictions of godly living (Mt 7:13).

As Enoch walked with God so must we: against the world if necessary (Rom 3:3–4). Yet God has also provided for us in this regard by gathering his people into believing communities, local churches where we are to meet regularly to encourage one another, to minister to one another's needs and to build one another up in the faith (1 Cor 12:7, 21, 25–6; 14:26; Heb 10:25). If we walk with God we will taste the bitterness of rejection by the world on account of our faith (Jn 15:18–21) but we will also know the comforts of fellow pilgrims who share with us one Lord, one faith, one baptism (2 Cor 1:5; Eph 4:3–6). These Hebrew followers of Christ had experienced rejection, isolation and loss for his sake, but they had God and one another and that was enough to ensure the victory of faith: 'You sympathised with those in prison and joyfully accepted the confiscation of your property, because you knew that you yourselves had better and lasting possessions' (Heb 10:34).

Those who walk with God not only recognise true from counterfeit riches, they also learn to distinguish between the small change of life and the things which are of supreme value (Mt 19:27–30).

Difficult places

If you walk with God you will often walk *in difficult places*. We must not romanticise the pilgrim's progress: it is not 'roses, roses all the way' but often a way of steep paths and sharp stones. God brings us into testing situations which challenge us but which are also the making of us (Rom 5:3, 4; Jas 1:4). A Chinese woman recently interviewed on a television programme on China had a severely handicapped ten-year-old son. She was only allowed one child and might have had this one aborted or worse, but she chose the harder path. There was nothing of bitterness or regret in her eyes but rather peace and serenity as she said, 'I made a hard decision but I would never wish to go back on it. I feel I am a more valuable person and I understand better what life is about. I am privileged.' So it is with the Christian. God does not promise to keep us *from* trouble but he does promise to be with us *in* trouble:

Fear not, He is with thee, O be not dismayed;
For he is thy God, and will still give thee aid:
He'll strengthen thee, help thee, and cause thee to stand,
Uphold by his righteous, omnipotent hand.

Richard Keen (1787)

Often those difficult places are in ourselves when God challenges our will, talks down our pride, uncovers our fear. Then we have to trust the hand that hurts us and the God who saves us – from ourselves! One thing is sure: wherever he leads us, God does not lead us carelessly or cruelly, but when life's path takes us through fire and water he can transform the experience from one of destructiveness to one from which we come out protected and refined (Is 43:2; 1 Pet 1:6–7). It is the work of faith to trust him in this and to go on trusting when only God makes sense.

High places

If you walk with God, however, you will also know what it is to walk *on high places*. What a privilege it is each day to open the greatest Book in the world and to find there our guidance, our comfort and our guarantee that we do not walk alone or in vain. What a joy it is to meet with

31

other Christians, brothers and sisters in the great family of God, and to sing with them his praises as a tiny but much-loved part of a glorious multitude in heaven as well as on earth (Rev 14: 2–3; 19:5–6). Above all, what a delight it is to be touched by God's Spirit in those times when his love is brought home to the heart in experiences too special and too exalted to be put in words; times of 'joy unspeakable and full of glory' (1 Pet 1:8). As the Apostle Peter notes, those times can come in persecution, hardship and undoubted sorrow. The high places can be in the hard places; the mountain-top experience can be in the deep valley.

I read with a wry smile the testimony of one Chinese pastor in a labour camp for his faith where he was put in charge of cleaning the latrines. He had to empty the contents of the latrines each day, in a field reserved for the purpose. The stench was so strong that the guards kept their distance as he spread the excrement on the field. This meant that out of earshot he could quietly sing hymns that were disallowed in the camp on pain of severest punishment and he records singing his favourite song on such occasions:

> I come to the garden alone
> While the dew is still on the roses(!).

He chose it because of its chorus:

> For he walks with me and he talks with me
> And he tells me that I am his own
> And the joy we share as we tarry there
> None other has ever known

All the way my Saviour leads me

It is possible to walk as Enoch walked. It is possible not only to know that there is a God but to know God for yourself and to walk with him in new life and joy and peace in believing. This is the life of faith, the walk of faith – and it begins at the foot of the cross. The end of Enoch's earthly walk with God was his translation to heaven: 'He did not experience death; he could not be found because God had taken him away' (Heb 11:5). The deliverance of Enoch from death is deeply significant, coming as it does in a record which shows how universal and inevitable death was after Adam and Eve's fall. It is a glimpse toward final possibilities which will be realised and exhibited fully only in the risen Christ long centuries later. In Christ's teaching but most of all in his own resurrection he has 'brought life and immortality to light' (2 Tim 1:10). His coming in general judgement will be the end of history and the climax to a long period of waiting and praying: 'Just as man is destined to die once, and after that to face judgement, so Christ was sacrificed once to take away the sins of many people; and he will appear a second time, not to bear sin, but to bring salvation to those who are waiting for him' (Heb 9:27–8).

The Apostle Jude tells us that Enoch looked forward to that day. He did not have the clarity of the New Testament revelation of course, yet Enoch too believed in and spoke to his generation of 'righteousness, self-control and judgement to come' (Acts 24:25) There has always been, deep in the human heart, an awareness of God and of judgement to come. Enoch addressed that, he foresaw and prepared for a coming judgement which would involve the populations of two worlds! 'See the Lord is coming with thousands upon thousands of his holy ones to judge everyone, and to convict all the ungodly of all the ungodly acts they have done in the ungodly way, and of all the harsh words ungodly sinners have spoken against him' (Jude 14–15, [quoted from the book of Enoch]).

Enoch and Noah both lived in a world of hard words where contempt towards godliness often found voice, a world which exists now as then (2 Pet 3:3–7). Jesus warned that such words were not lost on the wind but recorded in heaven to be recalled on the Day of Judgement (Mt

12:36). Their seriousness lies in the insult they offer to God's majesty and character and in the power they have to keep people from the kingdom of God. Words can do more than wound; they can damn. We live in an age of satire where nothing is sacred, an age in which believers need to have Enoch's vision of a final judgement when truth will be fully revealed and finally vindicated. Faith often has to walk through a storm of words – mocking, biting even lying words – and it can 'please God' even as it does so. So faith journeys through every landscape, walking with God whose company makes up for all the loneliness and loss: 'Even though I walk through the valley of the shadow of death, I will fear no evil, for you are with me... Surely goodness and love will follow me all the days of my life and I will dwell in the houses of the Lord for ever' (Ps 23:4, 6).

5

FAITH AND ITS REWARD

'*And without faith it is impossible to please God, because anyone who comes to him must believe that he exists and that he rewards those who earnestly seek him*' (Heb 11:6).

It is remarkable and tragic how ingeniously people marginalise God. Good people, decent people, unselfish people will be good, decent and unselfish without any reference to God and will even make a virtue of it. You will probably have heard of the ancient philosopher who was found walking around with a flaming torch in one hand and a bucket of water in the other. 'What are you doing,' they asked 'what do these things mean?' The reply came back: 'With this torch I am going to burn heaven and with this water I am going to extinguish hell. Then people will do good without hope of the one or fear of the other.' No doubt the old story has various forms and many origins. The philosophy seems to be one of dispassionate, unselfish service. But is it? And is it true? What is fundamentally wrong with it is that it marginalises God and his blessing. God becomes irrelevant and his promises are treated with disdain. It is not in fact a biblical concept at all.

Throughout this chapter we will discover men and women who do what they do with God in their hearts and his reward in their sights. We will meet Abraham, 'looking for a city whose architect and builder is God', Isaac who 'blessed Jacob and Esau in regard to their future', Moses who 'was looking ahead to his reward', and others who were tortured for their faith but 'refused to be released so that they might gain a better resurrection'. In fact we shall find all the pilgrims of Hebrews 11 'longing for a better country – a heavenly one', and we shall be assured that God 'has prepared a city for them' (Heb 11:16). We shall not find, however, a torch or a bucket in this or any other chapter of the Bible!

Jesus himself, by clear statements and parables, held out the reality and desirability of God's *reward* for faithful service. We have it in the parable of the talents (Mt 18:23–5), the parable of the sheep and the goats (Mt 25:31–46) and many others. He himself lived to please his Father (Jn 8:29) and he himself 'for the joy that was set before him endured the cross, scorning its shame and sat down at the right hand of the throne of God' (Heb 12:2; cf. Jn 17:5). This was his antidote to opposition and discouragement (Heb 12:3) and it can rightly be ours.

Faith is important

In verse five we read that Enoch's reward was that he was 'taken from this life' in such a manner that 'he did not experience death', and the thing for which he was so singularly honoured was that he 'pleased God' by a life of faith. For the writer of Hebrews, righteousness and faith are inseparable; no amount of good works can make up for faith in the true and living God because nothing can make up for him. So he writes, explaining Enoch's life and its rewards: 'And without faith it is impossible to please God' (Heb 11:6).

There are people who say airily, 'Oh, I don't concern myself with religion, I live the life. And anyway it's people who matter and how you treat them.' This may appear to give a high value to human beings, but in reality it loses sight of their highest quality and fittest destiny, for we get a full and sufficient evaluation of human worth and dignity only from God our creator who has made us in his image and for himself and who offers to share his endless life with us. Moreover, human nature being what it is, the claim 'I live the life' is generally questionable since however we value others we usually put ourselves on top of the list of our priorities. Certainly when we stand before God on the Day of Judgement, we shall all see sin for what it is and recognising its corrupting effect on our best works. Most of all, however, the claim that what you believe isn't important is really saying that *God* isn't important. It is a denial of his goodness in giving us life with all its values and blessings, and it is an insult to his majesty and honour in refusing to live for his glory and praise. God as creator is at the centre of all creation, even in its present damaged state, sustaining it and guiding it and he demands that he be given the central place as Lord in every human life. But it is precisely *there* that by nature we do not want him. As sinners we want that central place for ourselves! It matters *that* we believe and it also matters *what* we believe.

Faith has content

True faith, biblical faith, saving faith, has *content*: 'Anyone who comes to him must believe that he exists and that he rewards those who earnestly seek him' (Heb 11:6). Biblical faith is specific: it is faith in the one true God and an awareness of his love and grace. In the New Testament, faith is focused on Jesus Christ, God's perfect image (Heb 1:3) and the supreme object of faith for all who seek peace with God (Mt 28:19–20; Jn 12:32; Acts 4:12; Rom 5:1–2). His death as an atoning sacrifice for sin is central to the gospel (Mk 10:45; Rom 3:21–6; 1 Cor 2:1–5; Heb 10:11–14).

The content of faith is essential to its character as Christian faith. It is simply not true that 'any dream will do'. In his last epistles Paul leaves a legacy which stresses again and again the importance of true faith (1 Tim 1:15, 19), faith well-understood (4:11–16) and clearly defined (1 Tim 6:3; 2 Tim 4:2–5) and faith kept sound and safe for future generations: 'What you heard from me keep as the pattern of sound teaching with faith and love in Christ Jesus. Guard the good deposit that was entrusted to you – guard it with the help of the Holy Spirit who lives in us' (2 Tim 1:13–14).

There is a danger today, even in Christian circles, of minimising the content of faith and maximising 'spiritual experience' until faith itself becomes separated from its biblical roots. This might suit a New Age philosophy but it is incompatible with a New Covenant theology. A group of theologians met a few years back and published their findings for the larger good of the Church. They were very broad and liberal about a lot of things and came to the conclusion that it wasn't *what* you believed but *how* you believed that mattered. Now that sounds very good at first no doubt, but supposing I went home after a conference, was greeted by my wife with a long kiss at the door and the question 'Do you love me?' And supposing I answered, 'Oh my dear, I have learned that it's not *who* I love but *how* I love that matters.' I'd be outside the door pretty sharply!

God is a God of revelation. In love and mercy he has revealed himself clearly to our race. 'Prophecy,' says the Apostle Peter, 'never had its origin in the will of man, but men spoke from God as they were carried along by the Holy Spirit' (2 Pet 1:21). 'All Scripture,' says Paul, 'is God-breathed' (2 Tim 3:16). Supremely he has revealed himself in Jesus Christ, the Word made flesh (Jn 1:1, 14). However, by nature we are disposed to substitute God's word for our own, to question and reject his self-revelation, preferring our own ideas and philosophies. We pride ourselves on an independence the Bible condemns.

Unbelief is sin

In the Bible, atheism and even agnosticism is never regarded as an intellectual problem but as a personal rebellion. The Bible teaches that we are atheists in our hearts (Ps 53:1) before we become atheists in our heads. Unbelief is never something neutral (even in the 'humble agnostic'). Paul relates it to the 'hardening of our hearts' against the rights of God in our lives. Our stubborn rebellion and self-will has led to a hardening of our hearts and this in turn has led to a darkening of our understanding in the things of God. We have separated ourselves from the life of God and the life God wants us to live as a result. Undervaluing God, we devalue all of life: 'So I tell you this and insist on it in the Lord, that you must no longer live as the Gentiles do, in the futility of their thinking. They are darkened in their understanding and separated from the life of God because of the ignorance that is in them due to the hardening of their hearts' (Eph 4:18).

Whatever may be the personal code and lifestyle of some, it is all too plain in societies throughout history that pride, lust and greed have filled the space left by God's absence at the centre (Eph 4:19; 1 Jn 2:16). We use our intellects to defend our prejudices. We would rather have a universe without purpose than a creator with one. The novelist Aldous Huxley, in a moment of biographical confession, wrote these words in *Ends and Means*: 'I had motives for not wanting the world to have a meaning; consequently assumed that it had none and was able without any difficulty to find satisfying reasons for this assumption . . .[1] For myself, the philosophy of meaningless was essentially an instrument of liberation, sexual and political.' It has been like this in all civilisations since the Fall. Paul observes of many in his own society: 'Having lost all sensitivity, they have given themselves over to sensuality so as to indulge in every kind of impurity, with a continual lust for more' (Eph 3:19).

The Bible never tries to prove the existence of God; it everywhere assumes it – from its first sentence in Genesis 1:1 to its last in Revelation 22:21. This is not to be dismissed as evading the issue. It is we who evade the issue. The Scriptures never allow us to leave God at the end of the argument; they never allow us to occupy 'neutral ground' with regard to him. They tell us that God is in everything and every thought process, that the creator made us to understand and deduce his eternal power and divine nature from the created order; we are programmed to recognise God's signature in creation. They also tell us that we are 'without excuse' when we suppress the truth about God, when we confuse him with his creation, and when we put substitute loyalties in his place (Rom 1:18–25).

God is not waiting at the end of human enquiry. God is not the static object of our philosophical investigations. He does not lie down on the dissecting table of science or hide in shadows of mystery and magic. He is the God who has entered human history in speech and in flesh; he is the God who has spoken by the prophets and who has sent his Son; he is the God who approaches us in the gospels and says: 'This is my Son. Listen to him. Come to him for forgiveness and new life. Repent and turn. Love me and obey.' We do not challenge him. He challenges us!

There is a reward for faith

There is every encouragement for those who seek God and serve him. The life of faith that pleases God begins with the recognition of God and his character. It responds to his call and goes on, like Enoch, to walk in his company. This is possible only because of Jesus Christ who is for us 'wisdom from God' (1 Cor 1:30), whose revelation of the Father is perfect (Heb 1:1–2), whose atonement for sin is complete (Heb 1:3; 10:14), who calls us to walk with him 'bearing the despite he bore' and 'looking for the city that is to come' (Heb 13:13–14). It is ultimately only because of Jesus that we, any of us, can please God. Only of the perfect Son could the holy Father say: 'This is my Son whom I love: with him I am well pleased' (Mt 3:17). It is only because God was pleased with him that he can be pleased with us.

Yet now that we are reconciled to God by the death of his Son, we discover that we can please him in these present lives of ours as we live by faith and learn to walk in grateful obedience. More than that we learn that he 'rewards those who earnestly seek him' (Heb 11:6). William Lane tells us that the verb 'to seek out' (NIV: 'earnestly seek') 'denotes a singular determination to devote oneself to the service of God'.[2] It is clear both from this chapter and the entire epistle that the writer of

Hebrews is not viewing such faith as simply an act but as an ongoing dedication of oneself to God as Saviour and Lord (Heb 2:1; 3:1, 6, 18–19; 4:1–2, 11; 6:4–8, etc.). It is this that God rewards. But wait! Is it really biblical to talk of rewards? Doesn't Jesus himself tell us that even when we have done everything we were told to do, we should say, 'We are unworthy servants; we have only done our duty' (Lk 17:10). Doesn't Paul call himself 'the worst of sinners' (1 Tim 1:15; cf. 1 Cor 15:9)? Didn't he write whole epistles to argue that good works can't *merit* eternal life or favour with God? And didn't the protestant reformation oppose the idea of salvation by works? Certainly. As Philip Hughes put it: 'To imagine that faith is in itself meritorious or establishes a claim on God and his rewards is to do violence to the very concept of faith which is the response of total dependence on the grace and goodness of God.'[3]

We shall have a correct understanding of the doctrine of rewards when we recognise that God rewards his people for their good works not on the grounds of their righteousness, but purely from his free grace and for the sake of Christ who alone merited salvation and the everlasting favour of God. It is all of grace (Rom 11:6) since he who saved us by grace also prepared us for good works (Eph 2:8–10), put his Spirit in our hearts (Gal 5:22 ff) and works in us 'to will and to act' (Phil 2:13). Consequently, 'when God rewards our good works, he is rewarding his works and gifts in us, rather than our own works'.[4] Augustine said something similar long before the Reformation: 'It is his own gifts that God crowns not our merits.' He added, 'Not that the apostle meant to deny good works or to empty them of their value, because he says that God renders to everyone according to their works; but he would have works proceed from faith and not faith from works.'[5]

A generous God; a rich reward

Yet it remains true and abundantly clear in Scripture that God rewards those who earnestly seek him and who serve him and suffer loss for him. Jesus had a beatitude especially for those persecuted 'because of righteousness' and said: 'Blessed are you when people insult you, persecute you and falsely say all kinds of evil against you because of me. Rejoice and be glad because great is your reward in heaven, for in the same way they persecuted the prophets who were before you' (Mt 5:11–12).

Later he assured his followers:

He who receives you receives me and he who receives me receives the one who sent me. Anyone who receives a prophet because he is a prophet will receive a prophet's reward, and anyone who receives a righteous man because he is a righteous man will receive a righteous man's reward. And if anyone gives even a cup of cold water to one of these little ones because he is my disciple, I tell you the truth, he will certainly not lose his reward (Mt 10:40–2).

In the parable of the talents rewards for good and faithful service are at the heart of the lesson with its refrain: 'You have been faithful with a few things; I will put you in charge of many things. Come and share your master's happiness' (Mt 25:21, 23). The Apostle Paul is equally clear that 'each will be rewarded according to his own labour' (1 Cor 3:8) and urges the Colossian believers, not outstanding missionaries or martyrs but wives, husbands, children, fathers, slaves: 'Whatever you do, work at it with all your heart, as working for the Lord, not for men, since you know that you will receive an inheritance from the Lord as a reward' (Col 3:23–4).

The writer to the Hebrews has earlier urged those who had suffered and might still have to suffer: 'Do not throw away your confidence; it will be richly rewarded' (Heb 10:35), and the Apostle John writes in his second letter: 'Watch out that you do not lose what you have worked for, but that you may be rewarded fully' (2 Jn 8). You see then that while the New Testament everywhere says we are *saved* by grace it also clearly teaches that having been saved by grace we shall also be rewarded for works of faith and love by a delighted God who loves to bless and encourage his children.

What is the reward?

But let me ask you one last question. What is the nature of that reward? I believe the reward is basically more of God and more opportunity to serve him. Let me explain. Grace enlarges one's capacity for enjoying God. In heaven all will have the presence of God and the beatific vision of his glory, but some will have a larger capacity than others, a larger capacity to bear the glory of his face, and their eternal progress into the glory will be correspondingly in advance of others (though we shall all eternally advance).

I think Thomas Howard and J.I. Packer deal well with this matter of rewards when they write in *Christianity The True Humanisn*:

Two points must be made if we are to understand what the New Testament means when it promises rewards, as it often does, to servants of God. The first point is that the reward is always a gift of love to one who tried rather than payment of earnings to one who succeeded; it is loyal faithfulness rather than dazzling fruitfulness that is being rewarded ... The second point is that the reward consists, not of something different from the activity that qualified for it (as when academic achievement is rewarded by a money prize) but of that same activity in its perfected form. As when the wooer wins his lady his reward is just that life of fully expressing and receiving love to which their marriage opens the door, so the reward which the Father and the Son through the Spirit bestow on Christians is just more of their love and fellowship and generosity – in short more of themselves than those Christians ever knew on this earth.[6]

Meantime you and I are called upon to trust and obey, to remain faithful, to resist evil and to await the glory of the judgement which is approaching the whole world. On that day our faith will be vindicated and our labours rewarded; nothing that we have done or suffered will be in vain and anything we have lost or been denied in life will be more than made up by the one who says: 'Well done, good and faithful servant, enter into the joy of your Lord' (Mt 25:21).

6

FAITH LEARNING TO
FEAR (NOAH)

'*By faith Noah, when warned about things not yet seen, in holy fear built an ark to save his family. By his faith he condemned the world and became heir of the righteousness that comes by faith*' (Heb 11:7).

'Let us now praise famous men' says the Jewish book, Ecclesasticus;[1] but the writer of Hebrews in this chapter is saying, 'Let us now praise *faithful* men' for faith is more important by far than fame as we saw with Enoch. What we have here is not a glittering galaxy of stars from the world of entertainment, nor is it a roll-call of heroes from romantic but mythological times (Lk 17:26–7, 2 Pet 1:16). It is a tribute to real men and women who lived in the real world and one all too much like our own in which faith has to fight to survive and has to grasp hold of the promises of God against all appearances. Anyone can have faith in the probable but to have faith about the unseen and the improbable is true faith and will be victorious faith. And this was Noah's faith.

Faith in hard times

It is hard to live as a faithful, godly believer in a culture which is cynical, contemptuous and corrupt. But that was Noah's culture. It is harder still to speak of God to the kind of society where the sneer or the snarl are your only response from those you are trying to help and warn. But that was Noah's task (see 1 Pet 3:19–20; 2 Pet 2:5). And compared to that long weary and thankless time of faithful but fruitless witness, building the ark must have been a relief! Noah lived in hard times. The record tells us:

45

The Lord saw how great man's wickedness on the earth had become, and that every inclination of the thoughts of his heart was only evil all the time. The Lord was grieved that he had made man on the earth, and his heart was filled with pain ... the earth was corrupt in God's sight and was full of violence. (Gen 6:5–6, 11.)

It is important that we understand human depravity and widespread corruption as the background to the judgement that follows in Genesis, the catastrophe of the deluge, the flood. It is a distinguishing feature of the biblical story marking it out from others.

Other flood stories

There does seem to be some racial memory of a great flood which devastated human civilisation. Flood stories have been discovered among nearly all nations and tribes – from the Asian mainland to the North American continent. Totals of numbers known run as high as two hundred and seventy. The most important of them is the Babylonian account and also the Akkadian story and the Sumerian version of the Babylonian account. These were written about 3,500–3,700 years ago and they show some fascinating similarities with the Genesis account. However, and this is the important thing, these other accounts also show huge and decisive differences.

For instance, the Babylonian flood story and others are grossly polytheistic; they speak of many gods. The 'gods' themselves are gross: unstable and immoral, and in the Mesopotamian story the deluge comes as a result, not of sin and wickedness but because the human race had become very populous and the god Enlil could not sleep with all the noise going on in the world![2] From there on the differences multiply and I need not enumerate them.

Contrast this with the biblical account (e.g. Gen 6:5) with its stress on the holiness of God confronting the universal corruption of humankind. Holiness is the first and foremost characteristic of God in the Old Testament

– from it proceed the two corollaries of *love* and *wrath*: love towards what is good and compatible with his holiness and *wrath* towards what is corrupt and unholy in his universe. This is the most basic biblical teaching about the character and reality of the God who is there – he is not 'only love', he is utterly holy and consequently capable of moral discrimination and hence of holy wrath and righteous judgement.

A modern problem

Our popular humanism is only interested in the possibility of a loving 'God' of broad and bland benevolence, but that is the god of the Greeks not of the Christians or their Hebrew forebears. Our God is holy, not amoral. He cannot just 'love' everything and everyone indiscriminately and identically, and he does not. What doctor loves the germs as much as the patient? What kind of God loves the rapist just the same as the victim? True, there is held out the offer of forgiveness upon repentance for the worst of sinners, but the build-up of divine anger is very fearful. Those who will not have God as Saviour will meet him as Judge.

We see all this in Noah's day. He lived in bad times. Yet God kept 'a remnant' as he always has and will. Moreover, God made him 'a preacher of righteousness' (2 Pet 2:5) and gave his generation time to repent and the offer of mercy. For Noah it must have been a hard path to tread with few encouragements. He preached long years but never had a convert that we read about. He preached as long as the day of grace and opportunity lasted: but even the day of grace has an end. On the day Noah and the others entered the ark and the deluge came, we read in the Genesis account: 'Then the Lord shut him in.' The thud of the ark's great door is echoed in the New Testament when Jesus warns that there will be the closing of the doors at his Second Coming and a certain, unavoidable, inescapable judgement for those still outside (e.g. Mt 25:10, 30, 40; cf. Rev 22:11).

47

Listen to an old preacher's account of Noah's lonely faith in this unbelieving world:

It was no easy thing for him to build the ark amid the scoffing of his generation. Smart witticisms fell around him like hail. All the 'practical men' thought him a dreamy fool wasting his time while they prospered and made something of life ... for long years the wits laughed and the 'common sense' people wondered and the patient saint went on hammering and pitching at his ark. But one morning it began to rain; and by degrees somehow Noah did not seem quite such a fool. The jests would look rather different when the water got up to the knees of the jesters; and their sarcasms would stick in their throats as they drowned. So it is always. So it will be at the last Day.[3]

Faith in full obedience

The writer of the Hebrews is writing to believers who are going through hard times, treading a lonely path, suffering many losses for Jesus' sake. He writes of Noah, not so much to talk of the tragedy and catastrophe of the flood, as to talk of one man's extraordinary faith.

First, Noah heard the warning of God about what was to come and he believed it because of the one who declared it: 'His faith grasped the invisible things to come only because it grasped the Invisible Person.'[4] He was prepared to side with God against the whole world if necessary) and so 'through faith he put the whole world in the wrong' (NEB). Have you learned the possible necessity of that in your own life, or are you always hovering somewhere between the majority and God? Have you learned to say with Paul the Apostle 'What if some do not have faith. Does their lack of faith nullify God's faithfulness? Not at all! Let God be true, and every man a liar' (Rom 3:3–4). Decide whose side you will take, and if you are on God's side then speak out even if what you have to say is unpopular and resented. Noah heard and received the warnings as well as the promises. He believed the whole revelation given. The Bible is not always a comfortable book to read, and God, even though he is 'the God of all comfort' (2 Cor 1:3), is not only or always comforting. He is also the God who confronts, who challenges, who warns and even threatens. Among the hard sayings of Jesus are many which warn the world and the individual of judgement to come in terrible terms (e.g. Mk 9:42–8) – terms that can only be justified by the terrible realities they warn us of and seek to save us from. Jesus did not find Noah's history an embarrassment but a beacon of warning to his generation and to ours (Mt 24:37–9).

Second, having heard God's truth Noah obeyed God and proceeded 'in holy fear' to build the ark as God had directed. This is important to the writer since these Hebrew believers are being tempted away from their new faith in Jesus and need to hear the warnings of this letter and to fear God. A greater judgement than the Flood is coming upon the world – and they need to be ready for it if they are to survive it. Didn't Noah have good reason to 'fear'? Yes and so have we! True, this is not a servile terror, it is a 'holy fear'; it involves worshipful awe and holy reverence and respectful obedience. This is good, sensible downright fear; not rampant panic but as an ingredient of faith, in godly fear.

Should we fear God?

Do you know what this is in your own life? Do you know what it is to fear God? I do not know when I last heard someone described as 'God-fearing'. Do you have this 'holy fear' in your spiritual armoury? Be quite sure of this that it is an essential piece of your spiritual weaponry or at least of your survival kit in enemy territory. Do you know what it is to fear God? I sometimes hear people saying, 'Oh no, not that. That's not how I see him at all. God is love; there is no such thing as the wrath of God. Why should I fear? There's nothing to be afraid of in

49

God. What is there to fear?' Well, perhaps in their case very little – from their God at least; *their* God seems quite safe, quite easy to cope with, quite tame really.

But the God of the Bible is awesomely powerful and utterly just and unbearably holy, and only those whose folly was as great at their ignorance would find nothing in God to fear. Only toy lions are cuddly; the real thing is fearful. It is God in his holiness confronting us in our sinfulness which has the most terrible possibilities for us – for any of us: 'The lion has roared, who will not fear' cried an Old Testament prophet. Aslan is not a tame lion!

Isaiah knew it in theory before the year that King Uzziah died; but in that year he knew it in experience. 'In the year ... I saw the Lord ... Then I cried out, "I'm finished for I am unclean"' (Is 6:1, 5). Job knew it too when the judge of all the earth finally confronted and confounded him and Job cried, 'My ears had heard of you, but now my eyes have seen you. Therefore I despise myself and repent in dust and ashes' (Job 42:5–6). Even the sight of Jesus, God with us, so accessible to us, so familiar to us, even the sight of Jesus in the full glory of his holy majesty at the right hand of God so awed and overcame his friend and disciple John that he says, 'When I saw him, I fell at his feet as though dead' (Rev 1:17).

In every case it is sin that causes this dread, sin that cannot bear the light, the purity, the challenge; sin that cannot justify itself, guilt that reads its condemnation like a sentence of death. And in every case it is God who justifies, God who takes away sin, God in Christ who says, 'Do not be afraid.' But he only says it to those who do fear, who know they have reason enough in their sins to fear and who, when they hear his 'not guilty', when they are lifted to their feet out of the dust where self-abasement has laid them, are thereafter lost in wonder, love and praise.

And so we live our days in fear and relief, in concern not to anger God and in confidence that his love will never let us go; he is our friend but he will never be our

pal, he is safe and we are saved but we will never treat
him or his salvation lightly and so we will never lose it:

> Fear him ye saints and you will then
> Have nothing else to fear
> Make you his service your delight
> Your wants shall be his care.

An ark for all God's Noahs

Finally, Noah was saved, he and his family, to begin a new
stage in the human story. You know how the Genesis
account goes on to tell of the dreary and terrible year
when the ark and its cargo floated above universal death.
And you know how Noah and his family came out to start
again the life of the race. Alas it was far from a completely
new start. They brought something of the sin of the old
world into the new and the old sickness and rebellion
soon manifested itself. It was easier to wash the earth
clean of mankind than to wash sin from the heart of the
survivors and their children.

Yet God in grace and mercy promised never to repeat
a judgement on the scale of the great flood, and so began
again the history of redemption, the eventual emergence
of Israel and, in the fullness of time, the coming of
Immanuel.

But the long story isn't over. Still the earth is given up
to great evil, still there is rebellion and sin and unbelief.
And Christ and his Apostles warn us that a final judgement remains at the end of history of which Noah's Flood
is as a foretaste and a warning: 'The day of the Lord will
come like a thief. The heavens will disappear with a roar;
the elements will be destroyed by fire, and the earth and
everything in it will be laid bare' (2 Pet 3:10). This is the
future the world ignores but which the Church of God
knows is coming and about which it must warn the world
in each generation and be faithful. Let us live and speak
out faithfully. We may save more than Noah ever did for

we live in the age of opportunity, the day of salvation (2 Cor 6:2).

Building the ark in faith was a prophetic act then; living the life of faith is a prophetic act now. 'Since everything will be destroyed in this way, what kind of people ought you to be? You ought to live holy and godly lives as you look forward to the day of God and speed its coming' (2 Pet 3:11–12). Noah lived millennia before Christ came. Yet it was for Noah and the Old Testament believers no less than for us that Christ lived and died. For neither Noah nor you and I are saved because of our faith but because of the Son of God who lived the perfect life for us and had perfect faith for us and died the atoning death for us. 'Christ redeemed us from the curse of the law by becoming a curse for us, for it is written: "Cursed is everyone who is hung on a tree"' (Gal 3:13). All true faith connects us with the greater faith of Christ and with his full provision for sin and so like Noah we become heirs of the righteousness which is by faith: the righteousness of God in Christ for all who believe.

Christ Jesus is our ark now: big enough for the whole world, strong enough to withstand the shocks of life, the rising waters of death, and the upheavals of the last judgement. There is safety here in the Son of God, sent to be for us all the shelter, the salvation, that we so desperately needed; our ark and safe-passage into the new world that God has planned. From that ark we will emerge to inherit a new heaven and a new earth (Rev 21:1). For the end of God's plan is not destruction but renewal, and the rainbow hangs in the air as a sign and a promise of a new day coming, clear shining after rain, the home of righteousness (2 Pet 3:11–13).

7

FAITH AWARE OF ITS INHERITANCE (ABRAHAM)

By faith Abraham, when called to go to a place he would later receive as his inheritance, obeyed and went, even though he did not know where he was going. By faith he made his home in the promised land like a stranger in a foreign country; he lived in tents, as did Isaac and Jacob, who were heirs with him of the same promise. For he was looking forward to the city with foundations, whose architect and builder is God (Heb 11:8–10.)

For the writer to the Hebrews, Abraham is the supreme example of faith in the Old Testament. He is not alone in giving Abraham special honour. Isaiah in the Old Testament and James in the New Testament refer to him as 'the friend of God' (Is 41:8; Jas 2:23) and the Apostle Paul in Romans calls him the father of all who believe (Rom 4:16–17).

Now if he is the father of all who believe, including us, then as believers we too have begun the life of faith which he exemplified. Consequently, his experience is our instruction, his example is our inspiration and his goal, the city of God, is our goal. Just as human beings belonging to the same species as their forebears are part of the ongoing story of humanity, so men and women of faith are part of the ongoing story of the Bible and its new humanity in God. We must not forget that their God is our God, that this is our Book, that these are the cloud of witnesses who encourage us to be in our generation what they were in theirs. We share, then, Abraham's privilege, but we must take up Abraham's challenge too: the challenge of the man who believed God and obeyed.

The God who is with you

He lived (as Abram) with his father Terah, the head of the family, and with his brothers Nahor and Haran, his nephew Lot, and with his wife Sarai (later Sarah) in Ur of the Chaldees. Ur was the great cradle of ancient civilisation, situated in modern Iraq, a magnificient city of about three hundred thousand men, women and children, wealthy and sophisticated.

To Abraham in Ur the call of God came: 'Leave your country, your people and your father's household and go to the land I will show you (Gen 12:1). The biblical account emphasises the divine initiative. There is no indication that Abraham was different from others. He was most likely a moon-worshipper as were so many others in Ur which was an important centre of moon-worship. But God is the God who makes the first move; he takes the initiative. The history of the world would be dark indeed if it were otherwise.

God chose one man in that great and populous city: one man through whom he would begin a new stage in the plan of redemption which would reach the whole world in time. But it started with one man in the crowds: not with kings and royal families in Ur or anywhere else, for 'God chose the weak things of the world to shame the strong' (1 Cor 1:27). Here is the doctrine of election: its manifestation in Abraham and its motive in the promise that 'all peoples of the earth will be blessed through him' (Gen 12:3).

So God reaches the many through the one, and if the many are precious the one is crucial. We need to be aware of that in our own days. We have our eyes too much on the many and not enough on the one in this respect. We say, 'If only Christians can get into Parliament in sufficient numbers or on television often enough and for long enough; if only we can marshal numbers big enough and bold enough so that no one can ignore us; if only . . .' And such thinking can so dominate us that we feel that until then we can do nothing. We feel hopelessly outnumbered, outclassed and outgunned in our particular Ur of the Chaldees.

Abraham was only one; a tiny spark in a sea of darkness. Yet from that spark a flame would kindle and from that flame the fires would spread to the ends of the earth. And why? Because God had chosen him, God had confronted him, God had called him and he had obeyed.

The God who can use you

The readers of Hebrews too, rather like Abraham, had been told: 'Leave your country, your people and your father's household.' Christ had called them into the fullness to which the Old Testament era looked and pointed. Yet they were persecuted and despised as apostates who had left the true faith. They too lived like strangers in a foreign country. If they looked back they would see the attractions of the Old Covenant, greater by far than the glories of ancient Ur. Yet they had been called to something still greater: to a better covenant, founded on better promises (Heb 8:6), with Christ as the great high priest of the good things that are already here (Heb 9:11) as well as the rest that remains (Heb 4:9–11). Abraham rejoiced to see his day (Jn 8:56), and those who believe are Abraham's children in truth whether Jews or Gentiles (Gal 3:7–9; cf. Rom 4:11–12). They are only a few, a small discounted minority, yet they are also the first-fruits of a great harvest, the first generation of a world-wide kingdom. Let them not value themselves as the world valued them, nor as their fellow Jews valued them but as Christ valued them. Abraham was nothing in the present but he was God's secret for the future they are less than nothing in the world but they are God's seed-corn in the kingdom.

It was the same with other believers in the New Testament and it is the same with us now. In the strategy of God, we are in our own day where for instance the Thessalonian Christians were in theirs. Thessalonica, an important sea-port city in Paul's day, was situated just off the M1 of the Roman world – the Via Egnatia which connected three Roman provinces. The new church there might have seemed hopelessly small and unimportant yet to the Christians in such a strategic centre Paul wrote: 'The Lord's message rang out from you not only in Macedonia and Achaia – your faith in God has become known everywhere' (1 Thess 1:8). This confidence was not in the resources of man but in the purposes of God.

You too have been confronted by God and called by God and you too have believed God and responded to God. In the rush of the modern world with its preoccupations and its own idolatries you and others like you seem very small and unimportant. But the same God is at work, the same strategy is unfolding and achieving the same plan. And you are an essential part of that plan and strategy! Like Abraham you have received and responded to a call to new priorities, new loyalties and new behaviour (Gen 12:1; Mt 10: 37–8). Even if you were not called to move geographically, you were called to the journey of faith which begins 'in tents', in fragile and very temporary lives on earth, and ends in the city of God and the glory of God.

Where God may take you

God spoke and Abraham heard; God called and he came; God sent and he went out. God did not give Abraham any details. It was only a beginning. He called him to leave for an unknown and un-named land. Only the bare promise was given. Says our writer: 'He obeyed and went, even though he did not know where he was going.' I love the remark of one of the old Puritan writers on that statement: 'He did not know where he was going – but he knew *who* he was going *with*'! Isn't that the greatest factor? You may often wonder where life is taking you – to what job, what country, what future? No one can settle such questions in advance. But somehow they don't seem quite so pressing when you know that the sovereign God, a wise and loving Father is going to be with you wherever his providence takes you:

God holds the key of all unknown
And I am glad
If other hands should hold the key
Or if he trusted it to me
I might be sad.

What if tomorrow's cares were here
Without its rest?
I'd rather be unlocked the day
And as the hours swing open say
My will is best.

I cannot read His future plans
But this I know:
I have the smiling of His face,
And all the refuge of His grace,
While here below.[1]

Here is the genius and the power and the victory of faith.

Trust and obey

Faith is defined and summed up for us back in Genesis (15:6) like this: 'Abraham believed the Lord.' That is surely the most perfect definition of faith: faith is just 'believing God' – believing him because he can be trusted, believing where we cannot see or even fully understand. I love Martin Luther's bold words on this passage:

This is the glory of faith, simply not to know: not to know where you are going, not to know what you are doing, not to know what you must suffer, and with sense and intellect virtue and will, all alike made captive, to follow the naked voice of God ... Abraham with his obedience of faith shows the highest example of the evangelical life, because he left all and followed the Lord, preferring the word of God to everything else and loving it above all things; of his own free will a

57

pilgrim, and subject to the perils of life and death every hour of the day and night.

Notice how faith and obedience are always together here: Abraham believed and then immediately he 'obeyed and went'. People often say they 'believe' but it is not the faith that obeys. It is not true faith: it is merely opinion or sentiment, however strong. True faith, God-given faith, justifying faith, saving faith has within itself the energy and character of obedience, of life-long faithfulness to God. As James says, 'Faith without works is dead.'

Here, in Abraham, is the faith that works. You and I too must learn to march to God's orders, to go where he sends us, and even when he takes us only a step at a time to take that step in that time. Sometimes we have to go out under 'sealed orders' and each stage is only revealed to us as we finish the previous one. But we can 'trust and obey' in faith and joy, knowing the one who is faithful and true and who will accompany us from the first step to the last. I think that if it is possible to regret anything in heaven it will be that we did not more simply and more joyfully take God at his word.

How God may keep you waiting

We tend to read the story without gaps but there were, in fact, long delays in Abraham's life. For instance, it would be thirteen long years before Isaac was finally born. Furthermore, even though God said when Abraham finally arrived in Canaan 'To your offspring I will give this land' (Gen 12:7), Abraham 'made his home in the promised land like a stranger in a foreign country' (Gen 12:9). 'He lived in tents' as would his son Isaac and his grandson Jacob, and he died not owning a foot of the land promised to him except the plot of ground he purchased in which to bury his wife Sarah, years later!

There is an important lesson for us here. Many of God's cheques are post-dated. We expect blessing to follow hard on the heels of obedience. We want promise and fulfilment to come with very little space between. We are not good at waiting for ours is a society which strives to 'take the waiting out of wanting'. We pray – and we want the right answer by next week; we claim a promise – but if everything continues the same we quickly get discouraged and even resentful. We need to learn that we have been called to live the life of faith. Being a Christian is not simply an initial decision but an ongoing discipleship – and an unconditional one too. God's promises are rarely fulfilled quite as we expect them to be. All we are promised is that they will be fulfilled in us and for us. But when and how they are fulfilled is God's secret and you and I can well wait until the Day when the books are opened – *all* the books!

Meantime faith has to 'live in tents' and be a foreigner in society; here on sufferance and often looked upon as a little foolish. And so faith journeys, as it were, from Ur to Haran, from Haran to Canaan and then from Shechem to Bethel and towards the Negeb. For so Abraham journeyed, claiming everything but possessing nothing. Patience was tested, reason might have revolted but faith held on to the promise of God.

Here too is the glory of faith: that it can go so much further than reason; that it can press on when sight and sense give up. So don't be disillusioned by your difficulties and your humdrum life. God will fulfill his promises even if some of his cheques are post-dated. Their time too will come. And there is always money in the bank to cover them!

Our place in God's future

Abraham's status as an immigrant and an alien in Canaan had the effect of directing his attention to a future beyond Canaan or any of the civilisations of his time. He looked forward to a new order of things in God which would affect heaven and earth: the city of God. Why does our writer speak of it as a city which has foundations (v.10)? Probably because a tent-encampment such as Abraham lived in and presided over has no foundations; it is nomadic, temporary, even fragile. And Abraham was reminded throughout his life of the fragile, temporary, provisional nature of his existence. Therefore 'he looked forward' continually to what was permanent and strong and final in God who plans and builds for an eternal destiny.

Over nineteen centuries later, Jesus said he had not hoped in vain (Lk 13:28; Jn 8:56). The Old Testament believers became increasingly aware that God would not allow the relationship he had established with them in covenant love to end; that he would not allow even death to end it (Ps 16:11; Dan 12:2–3). The New Testament believers were told more clearly and with convincing demonstration by Christ that God would not allow bereavement to rob him every day and every hour of people who are precious to him (Jn 14:1–3, 19).

Abraham knew what we ourselves learn from the earliest chapters of the Bible that human beings are unique, that we were made by God and for God, and that our sin brought death into the race. However he could not have known how a just God, the judge of all the earth, could forgive sin and free us from the penalty of our sins. He could not have known then that God would give his own Son as a sacrifice of atonement for sin and that in one mighty act of redemption millions would be freed for eternal life. He saw only 'at a distance'; but we see 'our Saviour Christ Jesus who has destroyed death and has brought life and immortality to light through the gospel' (2 Tim 1:10). That is our privilege: to be living in the new thing God has done in one world in Christ Jesus. We are part of the fulfilment of God's promise to Abraham that through him the whole world would be blessed – for Christ came to the Jews, Abraham's descendants (Gal 3:16), and Christ has come to us. And you and I know that the kingdom of God has its foundations at Calvary: it is founded on who Christ Jesus is and what he has done by his atoning death (1 Cor 3:11).

The faith of the justified

Paul wrote nearly two thousand years after Abraham's call: 'What does Scripture say? "Abraham believed God, and it was credited to him as righteousness." ... So then he is the father of all who believe ... in order that righteousness might be credited to them' adding later 'The words "it was credited to him" were written not for him alone but also for us to whom God will credit righteousness – for us who believe in him who raised Jesus our Lord from the dead. He was delivered over to death for our sins and was raised to life for our justification' (Rom 4:3, 11, 23–5).

It is important for us not to misunderstand Paul at this point. He is not saying that Abraham earned salvation by his faith as a religious work. His whole argument in this part of Romans stresses that we are not justified by works. The crediting of Abraham's faith as righteousness means that God accounted to him a righteousness that did not inherently belong to him. He was justified *through faith* rather than by faith. His faith itself was not his righteousness but was the means by which he received the mercy of God which treated him as righteous. The true basis and ground of such a treatment would be revealed two thousand years later when Christ Jesus would become for us 'wisdom from God – that is, our righteousness, holiness and redemption' (1 Cor 1:30). His once-for-all act of atonement, says Paul, was good for Abraham and is good for us. Abraham's God is our God, Abraham's goal is our goal, we are fellow-pilgrims with him to the city of God of which someone greater than Abraham has said, 'I am going there to prepare a place for you' (Jn 14:3).

Do you belong to the city of God? Is your citizenship in heaven (Phil 3:20)? Are you looking forward to that city as someone who has a place reserved for them in it? Do you know where you are going? If so, you too can sing:

'For ever with the Lord'
Amen, so let it be
Life from the dead is in that word,
'Tis immortality.

Here in the body pent,
Absent from him I roam,
Yet nightly pitch my moving tent
A day's march nearer home.[2]

8

FAITH GRASPING THE PROMISES OF GOD (ABRAHAM AND SARAH)

By faith Abraham, even though he was past age – and Sarah herself was barren – was enabled to become a father because he considered him faithful who had made the promise. And so from this one man, and he as good as dead, came descendants, as numerous as the stars in the sky and as countless as the sand on the sea shore. (Heb 11:11–12.)

There was a great sorrow in Abraham's life as there is very often a great sorrow in the lives of believers. Sometimes wounds are the best counsellors and the best comforters of others too. Many of those I preach to Sunday by Sunday are young and strong and successful: they have many ambitions but few wounds, many possibilities but few crosses. God has given them much and withheld little; they get a good deal of what they ask for and a great deal of what they take for granted besides! But the time will come when, in one way or another, they will learn, as we all must, that we are fragile people in a fallen world where sin and sorrow deal us deep wounds at times. And in our lives we have to handle failure as well as success, losses as well as gains, and God's 'No' as well as his 'Yes'.

Yet in all of this we can be 'more than conquerors'. For God's best word to us in Christ is not 'No' but 'Yes' (2 Cor 1:20); not loss but gain, eternal gain (Mk 10:29–30); not barrenness but blessing beyond description and without end. This study is meant to help us to grasp this and be confident in God, come what may. The great sorrow in

Abraham's life and that of his beloved wife, was Sarah's inability to bear a child. What Abraham did about this and what God eventually did about it is the subject of this chapter and from it we will learn some more of the lessons concerning the life of faith.

God gives us promises

Abraham is given a wonderful vision of God and hears the blessing of God on his life: 'Do not be afraid, Abram. I am your shield, your very great reward' (Gen 15:1). Yet Abraham cannot but express the sorrow and anguish of his heart: 'O Sovereign Lord, what can you give me since I remain childless' (Gen 15:2). Even if he becomes a great nation it will, he fears, be only formally and through an adopted servant and not a son of his begetting (Gen 15:2–3). Then God in his goodness and mercy reveals to Abraham his plan:

> Then the word of the Lord came to him:
> 'This man will not be your heir, but a son coming from your own body will be your heir.' He took him outside and said, 'Look up at the heavens and count the stars – if indeed you can count them.' Then he said to him, 'So shall your offspring be.' (Gen 15:4–5.)

Notice this striking fact: God gave the promise in such a way that everytime Abraham looked up at the stars he would remember it and celebrate the goodness of God toward him: every night he would be reminded of the divine plan for him. Perhaps sometimes he would start to count – and give up with laughter. The stars in their courses would minister unfailing encouragement to him.

And no doubt he needed it – as you and I often need encouragement, even when God has come into our lives, even when he has blessed us. How easy it is to forget! How easy for impressions to fade and memory to dim. How easy to lose feelings and an experience even of God! We need our reminders, our night sky which is always there: studded with solid affirmations of God and his promises.

Yet we have, in fact, something more. We have the Scriptures which are better than the stars. Abraham had a silent witness, we have a talking Book. We have a Bible studded with the promises of God. Psalms that reflect our turmoil and radiate God's peace; histories that show us that the Lord reigns above the chaos; prophets who do not offer us their own ideas but the word of the Lord (1 Pet 1:20–1) and, more than the prophets, a Son who says, 'You believe in God: believe also in me. I am the truth, the light of the world, the shepherd of the sheep, the bright and morning star, the alpha and the omega.' As the sky is full of stars so our Bible is full of promises. Count them if you can; but trust them if you can't.

Learning to wait

I said in the previous chapter that many of God's cheques were post-dated. Many of the Old Testament saints had to wait long years before they received what was promised. Joseph waited twenty years for his prophetic dream to be fulfilled; Moses waited forty years before he would even begin the work he had set his heart on; David was anointed king-in-waiting by Samuel years before he sat on the throne of Judah and years more passed before he was acknowledged throughout the land and by the twelve tribes.

So also Abraham had to endure long years of delay and fading hopes. Ten years passed in Canaan with still no sign of a child for Sarah. And then she had an idea – she would have a child by proxy: 'Now Sarai, Abram's wife, had born him no children. But she had an Egyptian maid-servant named Hagar; so she said to Abram, "The Lord has kept me from having children. Go sleep with my maidservant; perhaps I can build a family through her"' (Gen 16:1–2).

There were of course no test-tube babies, but there could be surrogate mothers and Sarah's Egyptian maidservant, Hagar, might be just right for the purpose. Well, just right for Sarah's purpose perhaps, but not for God's. Do you know the result of this piece of manipulation on Sarah's part? It issued in a child, Ishmael, who became the ancestor of a desert race, the Ishmaelites, which became the centuries-long enemy of Israel (Ps 83:6).

God's work must be done in God's way or it will not receive God's blessing. Sadly it is possible to 'help' God's work in such a way as to compromise and even damage it. We can never further God's work by sin; God does not build on an unsafe foundation. And we can never strengthen the cause of God or achieve the true purposes of God by worldly methods and worldly compromise. When you corrupt the promises of God the promises themselves turn against you; when you bend the rules you break the blessing. God's work must be done in God's way.

Our natural tendency towards haste is a danger to us in these matters. There is a story told of Phillips Brooks (1835–93) the great American preacher and Bishop of Boston. One day a friend found the normally imperturbable preacher pacing up and down his study like a caged lion. 'What's the trouble, Dr Brooks?' asked the friend. 'The trouble is that I'm in a hurry, but God isn't?' Brooks replied. Our faith is often tested by God's delays but we must learn that his delays are not his denials. His timing is often mysterious because his purposes are vast and far-reaching; but were we touched by the eagerness and joy with which he views the fulfilment of his promises we would spend the waiting time more in praise and less in complaint. Meantime we can be comforted as well as chided as we turn the pages of this story of Abraham and Sarah and see God's wisdom triumph over human folly.

How good it is, however, to be able to turn the pages of Genesis and see God's wisdom triumph over our folly because God keeps his promises.

When Abraham was ninety-nine years old the Lord came to him in an awesome encounter, promised him again the land of Canaan and an entire nation of descendents to people it, and instituted the rite and mark of circumcision for all Hebrew males as a perpetual sign that the nation belonged to God.

Then, setting aside Sarah's earlier attempt to get an heir for Abraham by another woman, God further promises that Sarah (at ninety!) will become pregnant (there never was HRT like this!). She would become mother to Isaac and through him the 'mother of nations'. And Abraham 'fell face down; he laughed and said to himself, "Will a son be born to a man a hundred years old? Will Sarah bear a child at the age of ninety?"' (Gen 17:17). Our hero did not quite 'fall about laughing' as we use the phrase, but there is surely a mixture of emotions here: joy touched with incredulity; faith in two minds but faith nevertheless. In fact in these chapters we have a good deal of laughter of one sort and another: the laughter of joy and incredulity here in Genesis 17:17, the laughter of scorn soon regretted in Genesis 18:12ff, and finally the laughter of celebration as Isaac is born and named – a name which means 'he laughs' (see Gen 21:1–7).

Learning to trust

What lessons for us there are in all this: lessons in the promises of God which go far beyond our expectations; warnings about unbelief and manipulation; and lessons too in the triumph of God's goodness and grace and the laughter he brings into lives which, for all their failures, belong to him and will share in his blessing. Let us learn to trust the promises of God and build our entire lives on them come what may: God will keep his promises, that is his character. Abraham, says the writer of Hebrews, 'considered God faithful' and so must we. That great Victorian preacher C.H. Spurgeon used to say, 'If God had meant to run back from any promise, he would surely have run back from the promise to give his only begotten Son; but having fulfilled that, what promise is there that he will ever break?'[1]

I once read the story of a man who crossed the Mississippi on foot when it was frozen over. Half way across he lost confidence and began to panic. He finished his crossing crawling on his stomach, soaked and chilled. Imagine his face when almost immediately after standing on shore he saw another man, sitting on a large sled loaded with pig iron, wave cheerily as he passed and drive over in complete safety!

Now it will be like that for some Christians travelling through from earth to heaven supported 'only' on the promises of God. Some will go through their whole pilgrimage worried, fretting, hardly daring to believe that their God and Saviour can cope with their failures and doubts and fears and will keep them to the end. Others press on with confidence and even joy, sometimes slipping but regaining their foothold and pressing on: confident in God, determined to serve and love and obey him and praising him as if in prospect of glory.

Which are you? Do you act as if you were on thin ice or solid rock? The promises of God are as strong and sure as the God who made them! I can't get out of my mind the picture of that man crawling over a river covered with ice feet deep! It's like that with so many of us inching towards survival when we could be striding towards victory, creeping along our own pilgrim's progress when we could be moving in confidence and power through our society and generation, sharing our faith and telling others more boldly about Jesus and what he could do for them. When we come to stand before God I believe the thing we will most regret is that we didn't take him at his word more fully. His promises are not thin ice!

However, let us be sure to trust in the promises he has made not in promises he has not made. Biblical faith is not just a piece of positive thinking, nor is it 'naming and claiming' what *we* would like, what *we* want or what *we* decide we need. Biblical faith, true faith, is a response to revelation, a response to promises clearly made and specifically applied. Abraham did not claim an unpromised blessing and neither must we.

God will hear us and understand our pain when we say, as we can say to our Father, 'You have given me no children ... no successor ... no partner in life ... no relief from weakness or pain ... no converts', and he will love us and help us. He may not give us what we want, even what we most want in all the world, but he will give us himself: himself now in the tears and himself one day in the glory, where every tear will be wiped away; where 'there will be no more death or mourning or crying or pain' (Rev 21:4).

9

FAITH LOOKING FORWARD

All these people were still living by faith when they died. They did not receive the things promised; they only saw them and welcomed them from a distance. And they admitted that they were aliens and strangers on earth. People who say such things show that they are looking for a country of their own. If they had been thinking of the country they had left, they would have had opportunity to return. Instead, they were longing for a better country – a heavenly one. Therefore God is not ashamed to be called their God, for he has prepared a city for them. (Heb 11:13–16.)

Dying by faith

So far we have seen these great believers of the past living by faith; but what about dying by faith? Death is a terrible business; can faith meet it and deal with it? Our translation might give the impression that the writer of Hebrews is simply saying that these people lived by faith and then died; but his point is that having lived by faith they then faced death with the same faith. William Lane gives us a better translation when he renders verse 13: all these persons died *in accordance with the principle of faith*.[1] Philip Hughes understands it similarly and writes: 'Death with terrible finality disintegrates man as person, obliterating his faults and frustrating his ambitions; but faith, which triumphs over the vicissitudes of life, transcends also the negation of death ... the hour of death in particular is the hour of the victory of faith.'[2]

It is a great thing to live by faith and it is a great thing to die by faith and it is those who do the one who are sure to do the other. 'Our people die well,' said John Wesley.

71

'Blessed be God,' cried the Puritan leader John Preston on his death bed. 'I shall change my place but not my company.' It is true that doubts and fears can and do assault believers at such times of bodily and mental weakness and sometimes of pain. Then it is that faith must utterly rest on the character of God who cannot lie and who keeps his promises. 'Is your faith strong?' asked a pastor of a dying old lady from his flock. 'No, but my Jesus is,' she replied. She had learned the lesson of dying by faith!

All the leaders of Hebrews 11 were still living by faith when they died. They did not receive the things promised – but they did not doubt the promiser, and so although they only saw them 'from a distance' they welcomed (or 'saluted') them (Heb 11:13). The decisive and supreme thing was that God had promised those things. Again and again in this chapter and elsewhere in Hebrews we have references to the promises (Heb 11:9, 13, 17, 33, 39; cf. 4:1; 6:12, 17; 7:6; 8:6; 9:15; 10:23,36). The promises in view here are about three things in particular: the possession of Canaan (the 'promised' land); the foundation of a great nation by Abraham and Sarah; and the blessing of all peoples on earth through what Abraham would start (Gen 12:1–3).

These were great and glorious promises but the subsequent history of Abraham himself shows us how careful we must be in understanding God's ways, in not dictating to God *how* he fulfils his promises. It shows how we must be prepared to rest on the bare promise, the naked word of God, whether or not we feel anything or see anything come of it.

Our writer tells us that Abraham and Sarah and Isaac and Jacob lived and died 'without receiving the things promised' (Heb 11:13). Now that is nothing but a hard, inescapable fact. As we have seen, the only part of the promised land Abraham ever owned was the field where he buried his wife! Yet he did not die despairing or bitter or confused or unsteady. Why? Because he lived and died 'according to the principle of faith'. God had said it; he had received it; and he could rejoice in it and be sure of its eventual fulfilment. So he and the others saw and 'saluted' the things promised 'from a distance'.

They might be centuries ahead and indeed the 'city of God' in its fullness and perfection is still ahead even for us. Yet these things became sure and certain the moment that God promised them and we have something substantial the moment we receive and believe God in his promises: so faith becomes the demonstration and down-payment of what we do not yet see (Heb 11:1).

Believing is seeing

Throughout this chapter the forward-looking character of faith is highlighted. Yet it is not, thereby, a faith irrelevant to this world but one which directs us and sustains us in this present life. It is a main characteristic of true faith that it allows the future to shape the present, that it acts according to its expectations and 'stores up' for itself 'treasures in heaven' (Mt 6:20). This often seems a foolish gamble to people around us; but to us it is an investment in God that cannot fail. Ignore the scoffers who live for the main chance and miss the great certainty. They think your faith foolish *when you act on it*, when you live 'like a stranger in a foreign country' (Heb 11:9), when you become the odd one out living by impossible standards, basing your entire life on an improbable future. They say 'seeing is believing' but when you get the promise from a Christ who can be trusted and a God who cannot fail then believing is seeing (Jn 14:1–3).

Perhaps you live or work with people who mock your faith because they do not understand it; they do not understand it because they have not got it. Similarly they mock your expectations, your hope of heaven, your joy in prospect of eternity as 'pie in the sky when you die'. That is not surprising: the future does not belong to them, it belongs to us. They have to get all they can *out of* the present because for them the present is all there is. We are called to put all we can *into* the present because we have the future as well – endless, glorious, joyful. Because of this we can make a difference and the difference we can make is dramatic because we are not 'on the make' but having all things in Christ we can help those who are dragged down in life and fearful of the encroachment of trouble, age and disappointment.

Pilgrims passing through

Meanwhile, we are called to live like these heroes of faith who 'admitted that they were aliens and strangers on earth' (Heb 11:13), and all our earthly priorities, ambitions, gains and disappointments must be tempered by that. Meanwhile ... Ah there's the rub. What about the 'meanwhile'? Remember, our writer of Hebrews is stirring up discouraged or apathetic Christian Jews. They have left an age-old and honoured culture and religion for the new way; the way of Jesus as the promised Messiah – the Christ. But where is the kingdom and the power and the glory? They are weary pilgrims, trudging on in an inhospitable world despised alike by fellow Jews and unbelieving Gentiles.

Stop feeling sorry for yourselves, says our author. Stop hankering for the good old days and the grand old ways. Do you really know what the 'good old days' were in the time of 'father Abraham' and the others? They were 'aliens and strangers on the earth'. But, reply his listeners, they had their own land, the promised land, our homeland.

Yes but it wasn't enough! They were looking for something better than Mesopotamia or Canaan; they were looking forward to a city greater than Ur or future Jerusalem. They were looking beyond the present to the future; they were looking for a country 'of their own' (Heb 11:14), a better country (Heb 11:16) even than Canaan – 'a heavenly one'. And so they lived as 'ex-pats' wherever life took them and regarded themselves as 'different' from others who were content with this life – and even suffered for it 'Therefore God is not ashamed to

74

be called their God' (Heb 11:16). He is delighted with them; as a parent he is proud of them: they have the family likeness and they are on the way to the family home. Meanwhile: 'Every foreign land is native to them and every native land foreign territory ... they pass their days on earth but they hold citizenship in heaven.'[3]

The Apostle Peter has just such thoughts as these in mind when he writes to the believers 'scattered throughout Pontus, Galatia, Cappodocia, Asia and Bithynia' (five Roman provinces covering what is now Turkey) and calls them 'God's elect, strangers in the world' (1 Pet 1:1). The Greek word Peter uses for 'stranger' (*perepidemos*) means 'a temporary resident in a foreign place', 'a resident alien'. The word emphasises the temporary nature of the stay and there was a related term *paroikos* which indicated the legal status of the resident alien as a non-citizen. That last Greek word, *paroikos*, non-citizen, became a common term for the Christian community in a place and we get our English word 'parish' from it. I wonder how many worthy parishioners realise they are 'non-citizens'! That of course is also Paul's point when he writes to the Philippians: 'Our citizenship is in heaven. And we early await a Saviour from there, the Lord Jesus Christ, who by the power that enables him to bring everything under his control, will transform our lowly bodies so that they will be like his glorious body' (Phil 3:20–1).

As Abraham believed, even in his dying moments, for what he did not yet have, so must we if we are to live the life of faith for 'We live by faith, not by sight' (2 Cor 5:7). This always has been the essence of faith and it still is.

Not there yet!

Even in an age of fulfilment when Christ has come and the Spirit has been poured out richly on the whole church and not just on its patriarchs and prophets (Acts 2:16–18, 38–9), we still live 'between the times', between promise and fulfilment, between the world of sin, sickness and death and the future of 'glory, honour and immortality'.

In Paul's day some extreme charismatics in Corinth were forgetting that. They had turned theology into ideology and that into unreality. They even regarded the Apostle as having just got on to the lower rungs of the ladder which they were climbing so successfully. So Paul writes sardonically:

> Already you have all you want! Already you have become rich! You have become kings – and that without us! ... We are fools for Christ, but you are so wise in Christ! We are weak, but you are strong! You are honoured, we are dishonoured! To this very hour we go hungry and thirsty, we are in rags, we are brutally treated, we are homeless ... Up to this moment we have become the scum of the earth, the refuse of the world. (1 Cor 4:8, 10, 11, 13.)

Abraham of course did not have to go around in rags, he was in fact an extremely wealthy man, and you and I too for all our grumbles are not brutally treated and homeless because of our faith. However, all Abraham's riches were not enough to distract him from God's future. He lived in tents but had God sent him back to Ur of the Chaldees he would still have looked forward to 'the city with foundations whose architect and builder is God' (Heb 11:10). 'People who say such things,' says our writer, 'show that they are looking for a country of their own. If they had been thinking of the country they had left, they would have had opportunity to return. Instead they were longing for a better country – a heavenly one' (Heb 11:14–16).

No turning back

The Christians to whom this letter is addressed know the danger of thinking of that land from which they had gone out – that is, in their case, the Jewish religious and cultural and social milieu from which they have come in order to be followers of Jesus. They have indeed been tempted to turn back at times, like those of Abraham's descendants who perished in the wilderness between Egypt and Canaan (Heb 3:7–19); but to turn back is apostasy (Heb 6:4–8), and our writer, while warning them clearly, is 'confident of better things' in their case (Heb 6:9; cf. 10:39). They too have suffered as aliens, non-citizens, suspected and resented by Jew and Gentile alike. They have suffered insult, persecution and the confiscation of their property (Heb 10:32–5), but the examples of their great ancestors, Abraham, Isaac and Jacob are there to encourage and reassure them. Because they are willing to give up all for God, longing for a better country, better even than Canaan – a heavenly one, 'Therefore God is not ashamed to be called their God, for he has prepared a city for them' (Heb 11:16).

God is not ashamed of us

Surely we have here one of the most sparkling and reassuring statements in the Bible. Our faith at best is poor but it is faith in a great God rich in love. We have a God who is 'not ashamed' to be called our God. He sees that our faith is vulnerable and that we are liable at times to panic as Abraham did in Egypt and in Gerar when he lied (Gen 12:10–20; 20:1–18). Yet like a father seeing his child learn to walk, 'he is not ashamed to be called our God'. He has sent one who has made full atonement for Abraham's sin and ours. He has sent his Spirit into our hearts changing them, giving us new birth and the gift of true faith. He sees our struggles and knows our longings, he will help us and he will save us. He will take us to himself to heaven and into the future. He will not barely save us and hide us away in some heavenly attic. He sees what we shall one day be and he is not embarrassed, not ashamed to be called now, then and for all eternity 'our God'. And the proof is that he has prepared not an attic but a city and a new heaven and a new earth and a day of coming glory and final redemption. On that day the Lord Jesus will present to his Father a completed Church saying, 'Here am I and the children God has given me' (Heb 2:13). On that day God will be all in all (1 Cor 15:28), heaven will come down to earth and there will be no more distance between the two (Rev 21:1–3). From that day on and through all eternity we shall walk with God in unhindered communion, unspoiled service and endless glories. God lives in sight of that future therefore God is not ashamed to be called *our* God.

10

FAITH TESTED
AND TRIUMPHANT
(ABRAHAM AND ISAAC)

By faith Abraham, when God tested him, offered Isaac as a sacrifice. He who had received the promises was about to sacrifice his one and only son, even though God had said to him, 'It is through Isaac that your offspring will be reckoned.' Abraham reasoned that God could raise the dead, and figuratively speaking, he did receive Isaac back from death (Heb 11:17–19).

> Two men look out through the same bars.
> One sees the mud, and one the stars.[1]

In the story of God telling Abraham to offer up his son Isaac you can either focus on mud or on stars. You can say, as some have done, 'What a disgraceful, primitive idea! Child sacrifice? Horrible! How do you imagine God could be capable of such a thing?' Well, in actual fact God is not capable of 'such a thing'. In the Old Testament human sacrifice, practised by other tribes and nations around Israel, is abominated as vicious and corrupt. It brings down the wrath of an indignant God who is holy and loving and merciful. And in this story the critic might well reflect on the fact that God does *not* in fact allow it, nor did he have any intention of allowing it.

In Genesis chapter 22 we read that 'God tested Abraham' – and Abraham passed the test, not obeying out of slavish fear but in a profound and unbudging confidence that God would be true to him, to his own promises and to Isaac, the marvellous child of promise. Here are 'the stars' if we have eyes to see; a shining example of faith in

79

God which has never been forgotten. For centuries this story has been cherished by the Jews and for centuries it has been cherished by the Gentiles too (e.g. Jas 2:21-3). As a test of faith and as a triumph of faith it will never be repeated – but neither will it ever be forgotten. You and I have something to learn from this account; may God give us humility and wisdom to learn from it.

The mountain top is *in* the valley!

First of all, notice the time of the greatest test in Abraham's life. It was in Abraham's extreme old age, when he was well over a hundred and after many spiritual struggles and achievements. Don't ever feel that you've got the measure of God: that you can now predict what he will do with you, that your own course is set fair from now on for heaven without a hitch. Oswald Chambers puts it like this somewhere in one of his books:

A saint's life is in the hands of God like a bow and arrow in the hands of an archer. God is aiming at something the saint cannot see, and he stretches and strains and every now and again the saint says, 'I cannot stand any more.' God does not heed but goes on stretching till His purpose is in sight. Then he lets fly. Trust yourself in God's hands.

God may lead you into great trials and life may engulf you in terrible experiences, but always remember that the decisive thing is how you respond. The decisive victory of faith is won, not by getting *out* of trouble, nor even coming *through* the trouble but by holding fast to God *in* the trouble, come what may. That was Job's victory when he cried, 'Though he slay me yet will I trust him' (Job 13:15 AV). I have known believers of no outstanding piety make their greatest witness in such times; for them the mountain-top was *in* the valley. I think of the widow whose hard-working son lost his workshop and all his machines and tools in an arson attack, saying as he

80

returned home with the news, 'Thank God, Malcolm, that nothing can take the Lord away from you,' I think of the mother, having lost both a husband and a son who suffered slow and distressing deaths from cancerous tumours of the brain, staggering friends and medical staff with a tearful faith that said, 'The Lord gave and the Lord has taken away. Blessed be the name of the Lord' (Job 1:21). These were not 'great saints' but ordinary people who found extraordinary faith in hard times where God was near. They won the greatest victory of their lives in the darkest hour of those lives.

And that was Abraham's victory here: a victory won not on the way back from Moriah with Isaac safe but on the way to Moriah with Isaac given up to God. And so, the test, instead of breaking him brings him to the summit of his long walk with God.

'I surrender all'

Second, notice the test itself. It was not 'give me your millions' (and Abraham was a very rich man). It was not 'come and die' (which at his great age he would have been very ready to do). It was 'give me your son'. More still, it was 'give me your *only* son' (by Sarah). Nor is 'your only son' a reference simply to pedigree but to promise. There was another son, Ishmael, conceived by Sarah's maidservant at Sarah's request years before (Gen 16:1–2). But Ishmael was not the child of promise. Isaac was the only child that Abraham would have through whom the God-given promise would be fulfilled of descendants 'like the stars of the sky' for number and of a world blessed through Abraham's offspring (see Gen 12:1–3; 15:4–5; 17: 19).

It is just here that the essence and greatness of the test began. William Lane writes: 'When Abraham obeyed God's mandate to leave Ur, he simply gave up his past. But when he was summoned to Mount Moriah to deliver his own son to God, he was asked to surrender his future as well.'[2] Philip Hughes, another commentator, writes:

The sentence of death pronounced upon Isaac ... seemed in effect the sentence of death, also upon God's promise itself ... With Isaac dead the covenant dies too ... Abraham, however, as a man of faith held tenaciously to the conviction that what appeared to him an insoluble problem, was for God no problem at all. Though everything else was obscure, one thing was clear to him, namely, that God, whose word was unshakeably true, had a way of resolving the problem which was as yet unrevealed.[3]

We too must learn that God has a right to everything he has given us and to our lives as well. All souls are his; life is his to give and to take away; our gains and comforts come and they are good, but at any time he may require them or allow life to snatch them away. The only thing we will never lose is himself; the one guarantee which is absolute is 'Never will I leave you; never will I forsake you' (Heb 13:5).

Fear not, for I have redeemed you; I have summoned you by name; you are mine. When you pass through the waters, I will be with you; and when you pass through the rivers, they will not sweep over you. When you walk through the fire, you will not be burned, the flames will not set you ablaze. (Is 43:1–2.)

Faith triumphant

Thirdly, note the obedience of Abraham and its character. The account is extraordinarily plain and economical with words: 'Early in the morning Abraham got up and saddled his donkey. He took with him two of his servants and his son Isaac. When he had cut enough wood for the burnt offering, he set out for the place God had told him about' (Gen 22:3). There is no long and painful account of wrestling by night and tears by day; no cries for reprieve, no protestations, no delay even. It took three dreadful days and nights of travel to get to Mount Moriah according to verse 4. Abraham must have sacrificed his only son a hundred times in those three days. Yet so completely sure was he of God's faithfulness and that God's promises would be fulfilled, that, says the writer to Hebrews, 'Abraham reasoned that God could raise the dead' (Heb 11:19). Hence we read in the Genesis account, 'On the third day Abraham looked up and saw the place in the distance. He said to his servants, "Stay here with the donkey while I and the boy go over there. *We will worship and then we will come back to you*"' (Gen 22:4–5). Do you see it? He didn't say '*I* will come back' but '*we* will come back to you'. The writer of Hebrews explains such certainty as confidence in God's power and faithfulness even over death: 'Abraham reasoned that God could raise the dead.' What a faith! And to think that some Christian people don't read the Old Testament! This is Old Testament faith of a New Testament order. Abraham, so long before the developed doctrines of the Bible, has a resurrection faith!

And what of Isaac? I may have spoken of him as though he were a child in all this and so most of us picture him. But if Jewish tradition and Josephus are right, Isaac was about twenty-five years old and no passive and helpless figure. If so, then as the event develops and they climb the mountain together, father and son, and as he reaches the place of sacrifice and allows himself to be bound on the newly built altar, then Isaac too wins his place of honour in the patriarchal history and in the roll-call of great faith.

I said earlier that many express outrage at this story, but we should note that Abraham and Isaac are not among them. Those who protest fall far short of the faith and submission to God of the two main participants. Abraham did not revile God and Isaac did not protest: the critics will find no supporters there. I must say that it is the onlookers in great trials who are often those who protest and curse or question God; while often it is the sufferers who are the ones who conquer through faith.

And if Abraham ever conquered it was when he held up the knife ready to plunge it into the heart of the son he loved more than anything in the world – but not more than God. And at *that* point Isaac was offered up as surely as if the knife had descended.

'The Lord will provide'

Then, in the nick of time, while angels hold their breath, God calls out, 'Abraham! Abraham ... Do not lay a hand on the boy. Now I know that you fear God, because you have not withheld from me your son, your only son' (Gen 22:11–12). Then God provides, in place of Isaac, a ram caught by its horns in a nearby thicket, and Abraham called that place Jehovah Jireh, 'the Lord will Provide', and for generations it became a proverb in Israel that 'God will always provide on the mountain of the Lord' (Gen 22:14).

So the way of obedience may become the way of great hardship but it will also become the way of vindication and provision and blessing. When great faithfulness brings great loss, when faithful witness to Christ brings prejudice and scorn at work, and honesty misses all the boats; when obedience to God's call takes you far from home and the securities of a well-paid career; when at the end of faithful service there are few thanks and fewer comforts, then write these words on every blank page of the diary: 'The Lord will provide' (Gen 22: 14).

'The Lord will provide'! Write it over letters of disappointment turning you down for the job; write it over your bank statement when it suggests you can't give to the poor or to the Lord's work; write it over your anxieties, your fears and your failures and over your trials, yes and let it be written over your coffin too: 'The Lord will provide.' How he will do so is his business; obedience is your business.

Another father, another mountain

Finally we may find here the largest lesson of all. There was another Father who took his Son to another mountain, and together at Calvary, in a partnership more fateful and decisive than this, God in holy love gave up his only Son, Jesus Christ, the Lord from heaven, the Lord of glory, for the salvation of the world (Is 53:6–7, 10).

There was no reprieve at Calvary:

> We may not know; we cannot tell
> What pains he had to bear.
> But we believe it was for us
> He hung and suffered there.[4]

Yet there was supreme victory in apparent defeat, everlasting achievement in apparent wastage for 'God was reconciling the world to himself in Christ, not counting men's sins against them' (2 Cor 5:19).

There was a glorious return from God's Moriah too, when Christ ascended on high, the risen, victorious Lord, and led captivity captive, victor over sin and death and hell. The Old Testament scholar Gordon Wenham writes:

The New Testament writers develop this imagery in a very striking way. For them Abraham and Isaac are types [images] of God the Father and Jesus ... When Paul says 'If God is for us who is against us? He who did not spare his own Son but gave him up for us' (Rom 8:31–32), the echoes of Genesis 22:12,16, 'you have not withheld your son, your only child' are obvious. John 3:16, 'For God so loved the world that he gave his only Son', makes the same comparison.[5]

For us now, and for the Church for all time, the saying of Genesis 22:14 – 'On the mountain of the Lord it will be provided' is written in letters of gold over the cross of Calvary. 'The Lord will provide' has become 'The Lord has provided': a once-for-all atonement (Heb 10:10), a world-wide reconciliation (2 Cor 5:19), a full and free salvation.

The faith of Abraham may inspire us but it is the faith of Jesus that saves us, the Son who 'humbled himself and became obedient unto death – even death on a cross' (Phil 2:8). There is no atonement on Moriah but on Golgotha there is a once-for-all and perfect sacrifice for sin; it was what was done *there* that saves Abraham and Isaac and you and me.

11

FAITH AWARE OF GOD'S PLAN (ISAAC, JACOB AND JOSEPH)

By faith Isaac blessed Jacob and Esau in regard to their future. By faith Jacob, when he was dying, blessed each of Joseph's sons, and worshipped as he leaned on the top of his staff. By faith Joseph, when his end was near, spoke about the exodus of the Israelites from Egypt and gave instructions about his bones. (Heb 11:20–2.)

Of all the themes in the Bible there is one theme that runs like a golden thread from Genesis, the first book, to Revelation, the last. That theme is God's plan of salvation. It was first revealed when Adam and Eve were about to be expelled from the Garden of Eden (Gen 3:15); it will be fully revealed when millions of their race inherit the city of God and the new earth of Revelation 21 and 22. On the journey from the one event to the other, the purposes of God seem often to be lost under the debris of history, its chaos and its wars, its false religions and its universal failures. But it is only lost to sight. The river goes underground for a while and then re-emerges to flow on.

If there was one thing of which the family of Abraham was aware it was the plan of God which involved them, their descendants and the nations of the earth. However, they would discover that the plan would not always unfold in obvious ways. God is faithful but he is not predictable. His unpredictability is not however due to caprice but to his judgement on human sin: its pride, its self-confidence, its worldliness which seeks to use and manipulate even him! The patriarchs and their descendants had to learn that he is the God who is sovereign and free, whose election is inscrutable and who chooses 'the weak things of the world to shame the strong' (1 Cor 1:28).

Without him, to have Abraham for their father was nothing (cf. Mt 3:9) and to expect the blessing of Isaac to be sorely mistaken. Esau found that to be so and all his fury and frustration could not make it otherwise. The story of Isaac blessing his sons, Jacob and Esau is found in Genesis chapter 27, but to fully understand it we must look earlier into the characters of the three people concerned.

Isaac

Not all the men and women of faith in Hebrews 11 were great, though they were all caught up in something great which greatened them all. Isaac was a rather tame man it seems to me. If God had called Isaac from Ur of the Chaldees, instead of Abraham, he would, I think, have spent a lifetime packing his cases! He was not the great adventurer, the man of exploits, the initiator. His piety was passive more than active. He was passive, after all, in both of his two great moments: the one when he was born, the miraculous child of an aged mother, and the other when he was almost sacrificed by his father Abraham. I don't say he was not wonderfully co-operative in that last event, but he does seem to lack initiative and keenness of vision in his life as a whole; and in old age he presents rather a pathetic picture.

I may seem to be rather hard on Isaac, but I do have two rather serious charges to make against him in connection with the incident recorded here. The one is that he was insensitive to Esau's essentially irreligious nature and over-fond of him, and the other is that he tried to manipulate God by blessing the wrong son. I shall come back to that later. He was a man of faith and it was faith in God's purposes for his family and their descendants, but it was the faith of a traditionalist who knew how things should be done and could not quite stomach the idea that 'the elder shall serve the younger' (Gen 25:23).

Esau

You may be tempted to feel sorry for Esau, cheated as he was out of his expectations by a cleverer brother. But look a little deeper into his attitudes. He didn't just fall victim to a bad decision when earlier on he sold his birthright for a meal (Gen 25:27–34); he showed his scale of values, his priorities and his contempt of spiritual things. Later he compounded this when he married two Canaanite women, Judith the daughter of Beeri the Hittite and Basemath daughter of Elon the Hittite (Gen 26:34). These, we learn, 'were a source of grief to Isaac and Rebekah'. We learn more from Hebrews 12:16 which sums up his character as immoral and godless, 'who for a single meal sold his inheritance rights as the eldest son'. And the blessing and the birthright belonged together.

Jacob

Jacob was a man of contradictions. His character was devious yet he had a sense of spiritual things and a deep certainty of the all-importance of God. He knew how to grasp the main chance and capitalise on every opportunity. If you were marooned on a desert island and had to choose between these brothers as a companion-castaway you'd probably be better off with Esau and as regards a business partner you'd probably have been better off with Robert Maxwell!

Yet there is no doubt that God had chosen Jacob not Esau. That was or should have been clear from the start, for God had said while they were still in the womb, 'The older shall serve the younger' (Gen 25:23); Rebekah had always favoured Jacob and would certainly have told him the prophecy given before his birth. So he grew up knowing that he would be favoured above his brother. Yet instead of humbly trusting God for it he tried to 'help' God with his own scheming. He got what God had promised and what he had striven for – but he got it with severe penalties. He lost Rebekah (who was never to see her darling boy again). He lost his own home. He entered into fourteen years of exploitation and hardship for the woman he loved because her father was as cunning as Jacob. And the fear of his brother's wrath never left him.

The plan of God cannot be manipulated

Let us learn from Isaac's attempt to bless Esau that while he believed sincerely in the spiritiual power and significance of the blessing of God on his family and on their future generations his fault was that he tried to manipulate the blessing. Here is the flaw in his piety. When Isaac was old and his eyes were so weak that he could no longer see, he called for Esau his older son, 'that I may give you my blessing before I die' (Gen 27:4). But it was not *his* blessing but God's, and God had distinctly said the elder would serve the younger in terms of their descendants and the plan of God (Gen 25:21–3). Rebekah knew it and Jacob knew it and Isaac should have known it. But, alas, it was not only Isaac's physical eyes that were weak and he saw only the rites of custom, the law of primogeniture, not the election of God. He was cruelly deceived by his wife and his second son but only after he had spent years deceiving himself.

How easily we can do the same kind of things. Every parent wants to 'fix it' for their children. But we cannot believe for them or somehow get a place in heaven for them. Only one person can do that (Jn 14:3, 6) and only for those who trust in him. Often in a family there will be one child determined to find God with or without encouragement. They may not be the cleverest or the most admired of the family but they are 'different'. Jacob was one of those: he heard the promise and determined to grasp it and possess it.

And so Jacob, disguised as Esau, receives the blessing for himself and his descendants just as God had planned but not in the way that God could have opened up. As for Isaac and Esau, Isaac ends his life defeated, humiliated and convicted: 'I blessed him – and indeed he will be blessed' (Gen 27:33). Yet he finally surrenders to God's purpose: 'May God Almighty bless you and make you fruitful and increase your numbers until you become a community of peoples. May he give you and your descendants the blessing of Abraham, so that you may take possession of the land where you now live as an alien, the land God gave to Abraham' (Gen 28:3–4).

You see, Isaac really is a man of faith notwithstanding all his failings. He is in the line of Abraham his father and Jacob his son: and so he confesses the sovereignty of God in election and blessing. There is a lesser blessing for Esau which he gives but it is very earthbound – like Esau himself! (Gen 27:38–40.)

Are you Jacob or Esau?

Well, that is the story. But let me ask you which of its characters do you identify with. Are you Jacob or Esau? What does the blessing of God mean to you? These two boys grew up in a unique family called and blessed by God himself, the one and only true God. To the one it was part of life – to the other it was life itself. Where is God in *your* life? Is he simply in your background, taken for granted but only dimly known, or is he in the foreground beckoning, dominating, exciting, delighting.

Are you Esau, who sold his birthright for a simple meal because he valued the least of earth's blessings above the greatest of heaven's gifts? Your own brand of stew may be different, it may be your career, your love-life, your material comfort and status, but are you selling-out for it, abandoning an eternal blessing for a time-bound ambition? Or are you Jacob, rejoicing in the election of God who often chooses the unexpected and the unpromising (1 Cor 1:26–31) and who does not choose us because of anything in us (Rom 9:10–15) but who brings us to Christ, 'the mirror of our election', and who invites us to see in him our election and calling and to rejoice in them (Eph 1:3–6)? The plan of God cannot be manipulated but it can be recognised. Second, let us learn from Jacob's own experience later that:

The plan of God cannot be taken for granted

Ironically, Jacob himself saw history repeated when he, too, was an old man dying in a far off land – Egypt. The whole family had been saved by a son and brother thought to be long dead, that is, Joseph. Like Jacob, Joseph was told early of his special place in God's plan in prophetic dreams (Gen 37:1–12). And despite his own naïvety and his brothers' malice, despite the injustices of his life and its unexpected fortunes, Joseph does end up as prime minister of Egypt, second only to Pharaoh, and the brothers do end up bowing to him in awe and fear and he saves his family from famine and death and for a promised future (Gen 45:1–11).

The scene recalled by the writer of Hebrews is of Jacob's dying in Egypt some years after the family's removal there and Joseph bringing his two sons, Manasseh the elder and Ephraim the younger, for the old man's blessing (Gen 48:1–20). Carefully they are arranged at his right side and his left. Once more the law of primogeniture, the 'rights' of the first-born, is invoked. And then the God who took Isaac by surprise takes Jacob by surprise too. The Spirit constrains the old man to reach out in right hand and left hand blessing – *and to cross hands* (Gen 48:14) so that the greater blessing goes to the younger, Ephraim, and not the elder, Manasseh, and Joseph the prime minister discovers he is not the prime mover where God is concerned (Gen 48:17–19)! So we read of Jacob: 'He blessed them that day and said, "In your name will Israel pronounce this blessing: 'May God make you like Ephraim and Manasseh.'" So he put Ephraim ahead of Manasseh' (Gen 48:20).

Let us all learn the lessons of the crossed hands of God. The crossed hands of God continually surprise us. They often bless, even in the family of God, surprising people, and God makes unexpected choices in the people he uses.

He does more through Ephraim than Manasseh. For instance, he chooses David above his brothers. They have impressive talents but the Lord looks not upon the outward appearance but on the heart. One day he will choose a persecutor to become an apostle (1 Cor 15:9). Don't say God won't do much with you – and don't say God won't do much with other people! You never know how God will do his work. We look to Manasseh and God does a greater work through Ephraim. We look to the strong and God uses the weak. This has been God's way in history with nations, movements and individuals. The world looked to the great civilisations and cultures of Egypt, Greece and Rome; but God chose little Israel. The Church today must learn this lesson as God does more in 'third world' countries, even under oppresive régimes, than in the West with all its freedom and advantages.

The plan of God cannot fail

Years pass and Joseph himself is an old man now (Gen 50:22–3). Israel is still in Egypt but does not belong there! Joseph is great there but God has a greater place for him in heaven and even on earth. Joseph believes the promises of God for the future and gives his instructions:

> 'I am about to die but God will surely come to your aid and take you up out of this land to the land he promised on oath to Abraham, Isaac and Jacob.' And Joseph made the sons of Israel swear an oath and said, 'God will surely come to your aid, and then you must carry my bones up from this place' (Gen 50:24–5).

What Joseph does not know, however, is that his people must wait generations, even centuries, for the promises to come true. But Joseph knows that God keeps his word.

Don't judge God on the short term. One thousand years with him is as a day. Like Joseph we can be sure of God's future and therefore of our future for these are one in Jesus Christ. That future may seem less substantial than the present but it will be real and glorious when the pyramids of Egypt are dust and the empires of men forgotten.

Joseph had reached 'the top' in Egypt but yet he knew he did not belong there, he belonged to God and to God's future. So we may well get to the top or at least achieve something of status or wealth or honour in this present set-up; but God has something so much better for us that we cannot and must not say, 'This is my rest.' Egypt, even at its best and most hospitable, is still Egypt, the world is still the world (1 Jn 2:15–17) and our final destiny is the heavenly Jerusalem and the new heaven and earth. Let us therefore 'use the things of the world, as if not engrossed in them. For this world in its present form is passing away' (1 Cor 7:31) and with it its boardroom pharaohs, its changing prime ministers and glittering stars, its darlings and its drudges. Let us be grateful 'for receiving a kingdom that cannot be shaken' (Heb 12:28).

God's plan and our lives

Here are three stories about people who made plans. They didn't leave God out of their plans; on the contrary he was central to them. Indeed they were making serious attempts to follow and take forward his plans and not merely their own. Yet each of them found that even when they were at their most 'devout' still God's thoughts were not their thoughts (Is 55:8). They were each of them humbled as they tried to make God 'fit' with their expectations.

So we must learn that we can rarely read the small print in God's forward planner. We see the outline, we get the formal drift, we catch the general direction – and think we can plot its course, predict the next move, and be there, waiting, at the next stopping place.

I once heard it put like this. God begins to unfold his plans for us. He takes us to A and we are surprised; then he takes us to B and we are pleased; then he takes us to C and we are delighted because we can see what's happening. In our zeal for him (and for ourselves) we rush on to J, K and L. Then everything falls apart and we have to be gently but firmly taken back to D. You can't second-guess God, you can only go a step at a time. For you that is the step that matters. Indeed you have no guarantee that there will be a further step. That may be someone else's story. What matters most is that God's will is done at that particular stage. He alone knows the whole story because it's his story, a 'his story' within history and one whose end is sure and whose end is glorious. By faith we can look forward to that end and humbly play our part in its coming to pass. That part may be an unexpected one: we look in one direction and God uses us in another, we pray for one and another is blessed and used. Yet our own place in the plan is no less crucial. We are a link in the chain, that is our privilege, but remember – only God can forge the next link.

12

FAITH MAKING ITS CHOICE (MOSES)

By faith Moses' parents hid him for three months after he was born, because they saw he was no ordinary child, and they were not afraid of the king's edict. By faith Moses, when he had grown up, refused to be known as the son of Pharaoh's daughter. He chose to be ill-treated along with the people of God rather than to enjoy the pleasures of sin for a short time. He regarded disgrace for the sake of Christ as of greater value than the treasures of Egypt, because he was looking ahead to his reward. By faith he left Egypt, not fearing the king's anger; he persevered because he saw him who is invisible (Heb 11:23–7).

In Hebrews 11 we move from Joseph to Moses in just two verses but historically they were separated by centuries. In those centuries the family of Jacob became the tribes of Israel and flourished in Egypt. However, eventually, 'a new king who did not know about Joseph came to power in Egypt' (Ex 1:8) and the fortunes of Israel changed again. The Egyptian hierarchy became fearful of this populous and singular nation in its midst and to prevent any possibility of a take-over withdrew their privileges and eventually made slaves of them all. The Israelites entered a long period when the promises given to their forefather Abraham must have seemed remote and unlikely.

God in the dark

God had said to Jacob centuries before, 'Don't be afraid to go down to Egypt, for I will there make of you a great nation' (Gen 46:3). But what if Jacob could have seen the growing poverty and disgrace, the discrimination and the injustice, the slavery and the infanticide? The groans of Israel seemed to make a mockery of the promise of God and many must have said in the words of a later prophet: 'Truly you are a God who hides yourself' (Is 45:15).

It is a familiar predicament in every generation including our own. How can we make sense of the world when peace turns to war; when justice falls before tyranny; when the good suffer and the evil flourish; when Pharaoh's soldiers or Mao's Red Guards rampage and destroy. How can we justify God's sovereignty and trace the path of his wise and good providence in such a world as ours?

We live in a world conditioned by sin and the fall from God. By definition you cannot make sense of sin or its results, for sin does not make sense: sin is chaos, waste, cruelty, injustice, pain. What we can do is to hear God's word of reassurance and wait for his own deliverance and vindication. It is here that faith shows its powers and its strength. For faith can trust where it cannot track the ways of God. Faith can rest on the lone word of the God who can be trusted, the God who is good and who does good. Faith can see in the dark: not the whole landscape, sometimes not even the pitfalls ahead, but the light that shines and calls and waits and cheers.

It is the way of the world, sin and Satan to act as though God were irrelevant and then to pronounce him to be so! But God does not hurry to justify or vindicate himself, he does not let sin dictate what he does or when but he works in his own way and time – often hidden, frequently mysterious, but ineffably good. Trust him! Meantime he is not unaware of an Israel-in-Egypt situation. He has not only lived *with* the world's pain but *in* it, and on Calvary he has borne more than all of it together as 'the wages of sin'. As P.T. Forsyth once put it 'The cross of Christ is God's only self-justification in such a world as ours.'[1]

Key parents, key people

Moses was born at Israel's lowest point (Ex 1:13–14, 22). God does not wait for favourable opportunities, he makes them! In the valley of trouble he sets a door of hope. In Egypt everything seemed the same after Moses' birth as before (and indeed for most of a long lifetime after). Yet, in truth, nothing was the same. God had begun a new work; the new future was growing in the old present. First we have little people with a large significance, Amram and Jochabed (Ex 6:20). They simply believed this child had a special significance (Heb 11:23). There are 'key people' in the Bible but there are key parents too. Amram and Jochabed are the early creditors of Moses – he owed more to them than to Pharaoh's daughter. There are many other examples in Scripture. The prophet Samuel's mother gave him to the Lord before he gave himself to the Lord. Timothy knew the Scriptures through his mother Eunice and his grandmother Lois before he knew them through his great mentor Paul. And the story of many more is written in heaven.

Many people marvelled that so soon after the collapse of communism the Russian churches could be filled with worshippers who, it was thought, had had no 'background' of any sort of faith. Then they heard about the Russian grandmother in every family, the *Baboushka* who, while parents were out working or attending 'party meetings', quietly taught the young children about God and prayer. What could Stalin and his successors do about these – an army as undefeatable as it was effective in undermining the foundations of totalitarian atheism. You may not think of yourself as a key person but you may be a key parent – or, for that matter, a key grandparent, teacher, neighbour or friend; a crucial link in a very long and winding chain of faith and prayer, and light and truth in a very dark and precarious world.

So it was with Amram and Jochabed. By their response Moses is rescued from a programme of genocide. It was not to be the last 'ultimate solution'. Imagine the human situation, the grief, the anguish, the anger throughout the Hebrew settlements in Goshen; the jealousy that one baby should live when so many others had died and the corresponding threat of exposure even perhaps from *within* the Israelite settlement. There have often been such cases. Soon they can hide him no longer and so we read:

> When she could hide him no longer, she got a papyrus basket for him and coated it with tar and pitch. Then she placed the child in it and put it among the reeds along the bank of the Nile. His sister stood at a distance to see what would happen to him (Ex 2:3–4).

Alan Cole says that many similar ancient stories show:

> that this was a favourite way of abandoning babies in the ancient world. It was in fact the ancient equivalent of leaving them on the steps of an orphanage or hospital today. The shallows of a river near any Asian village would be the ideal place today to expose a baby and ensure its being found by the women who came to wash clothes or prepare food.

He also says of Pharaoh's daughter: 'If the Pharaoh in question was Rameses II he had close on sixty daughters. He also had numerous "hunting lodges" scattered over the delta area ... so there is no need to assume that Moses' parents lived near the capital Zoan.'[2]

Moses is hidden in a cradle in the reeds of the Nile. The spot is obviously a private but known bathing spot for one of the royal princesses. So Moses is found by Pharaoh's daughter who, guided by his sister Miriam, engages his Hebrew mother as a nurse throughout his earliest years. I think it was Ignatius Loyola, the sixteenth-century Jesuit leader, who used to say, 'Give me a child for the first seven years and I have him for ever.' Jochabed, by those early years, had Moses for God and Israel 'for ever' and all the perfumes and lotions in Pharaoh's court could not take off him the smell of the Hebrews and the mark of God.

God's laughter

And so it was that Moses was educated as an Egyptian princeling. The New Testament says he was 'educated in all the wisdom of the Egyptians' (Acts 7:22): its culture and commerce, its literary attainments and administrative skills, its politics and its international diplomacy. In linguistics he would have known Hebrew from his early childhood, Egyptian from his adopted family and schooling, and Aramaic the more general 'lingua franca' of diplomacy.

Think of it! Here God provides a literary and legal education for Israel's future law-giver (under God) and recorder of her earliest history. So God once again laughs at kings (Ps 2:1–2, 4). Two unimportant peasant-slaves act in faith and for forty years Egypt's greatest threat grows up in its midst and in a place of royal favour. The man who was destined to confront, to humble and to defeat one Pharaoh is reared in the royal circle of another!

Could Amran and Jochabed have foreseen this? No. But you never know what, in heaven, will be recorded as your finest moment. It may not be accompanied with great publicity or even with great satisfaction. It may be an act or a word, a stand against wrong or a sacrifice for right, a piece of faithful service given in weariness and soon forgotten, which will prove to be crucial in a larger strategy and a greater victory, one in which you did not dream of having part. What surprises there will be on the last day when God gives his rewards (Mt 6:4, 6, 18; 10:42), and Jesus his 'Well done' (Mt 25:40). Finally we have:

Moses' choice

There came a time when Moses had to make the greatest decision of his life. Whether to side with the Egyptian establishment or the Hebrew slaves. In the words of

101

Hebrews: 'He chose to be ill-treated along with the people of God rather than to enjoy the pleasures of sin for a short time' (Heb 11:25). Many would think he chose to surrender privilege – but in fact he chose a privilege that was held out to him from another direction, and a far greater privilege than any the pharaohs had to offer. So we read: 'He regarded disgrace for the sake of Christ as of greater value than the treasures of Egypt, because he was looking ahead to his reward' (Heb 11:26). He chose the real bargain! G. A. F. Knight has put it well: 'Whatever Moses' social position if he had remained on as a member of Egyptian society all we would know of him now would be as a name on a mummy in the British Museum.'[3]

In Os Guiness's book *The Grave-digger File*,[4] among the memorable illustrations by Nick Butterworth is a three-part cartoon which shows a rickety-looking 'Noah's Ark' being approached by a modern ocean-going liner. In the second drawing a line of people are walking up a gang plank put between the two boats while the captain is represented as saying 'Welcome aboard – not a moment too soon by the look of that old tub'! The last frame has the liner moving away and showing its name as it does so – 'SS *Titanic*'!

Today we are invited to abandon an old-fashioned and 'outworn faith', with its unbelievable doctrines and its restrictive morality, and enter the 'real world' of modernity with its secular humanism and its moral 'freedoms'. As ever, Egypt has so much to offer. Why suffer so much self-restriction and disadvantage in journeying to an unseen promised land when you can stay here and have everything – for a price and for a while? Why stay in the ark when you can side with all the best people in the *Titanic*? How poorly the Church seems to compare with the world at times: in culture, in talent, in world-shaping significance. But the people of God have been told of icebergs ahead, of failure and confusion, of calamity and eternal loss (Rev 18:1–24). However sophisticated, however resourceful, a society without God will founder on its own godless rebellion and selfishness and under the final judgement of God: 'For this world in its present form is passing away' (1 Cor 7:31; cf. 1 Jn 2:15–17).

Your choice

Moses' choice mirrors our choice in essential ways. He of course was born into the people of God and adopted into Egypt whereas we are born in Egypt and adopted into the people of God. Yet we too face a choice between the way of God and the ways of the world. We are familiar with the latter: its priorities, its way of working, its evasions and manipulations. But the way of the Hebrews' God is different, commanding new allegiances, new priorities, new lifestyles. It involves a dramatic new way of life: loving God with all your heart and your neighbour as yourself (Mt 22:37–9).

Dietrich Bonhoffer used to speak bitingly of 'cheap grace'. It is always a popular commodity in the religious supermarket: conversion without commitment, a change of mind without a change of life, hope of a place in the promised land without the need to leave Pharaoh's court.

The passage in Hebrews is full of the vocabulary of choice and commitment. The choice has to be made: not simply in our *thinking* but in our *doing*. Moses' choice was decisive and affected his entire life: he 'refused' to be known as the son of Pharaoh's daughter, he 'chose' to be ill-treated along with the people of God, he 'regarded' disgrace for the sake of Christ as of greater value than the treasures of Egypt, and by faith he 'left' Egypt and 'persevered' through long years of obscurity in Midian.

So we must ask ourselves what difference our 'choice' for Christ has made to our lives. Has it affected our careers, our involvements, our lifestyles, our choices? C.S. Lewis in his *Screwtape Letters* has a senior devil instructing a junior devil in the act of subtle temptation and at one point says in respect of the Christian facing new commitment:

The great thing is to prevent his doing anything. As long as he does not convert it into action, it does not matter how much he thinks about this new repentance. Let the little brute wallow in it ... Let him do anything but act. No amount of piety in his imagination and affections will harm us if we can keep it out of his will ... The more often he feels without acting, the less he will be able ever to act, and, in the long run, the less he will be able to feel.[5]

There are always reasons for staying in Egypt. The story is told that in the great eighteenth-century revival one of the new 'converts' was unwilling to leave an occupation out of keeping with his new faith. 'But Mr Wesley,' he protested, 'a man must live.' 'Yes sir,' replied the old evangelist, 'and a man must die.'

Going on going on

Of Moses, in the long years of exile following his decision, we read: 'He persevered because he saw him who is invisible' (Heb 11:27). It's been said that some people never count the cost and other people never stop counting the cost! They imagine that having done something for God he will now do everything for them and when things don't work out as they expected or hoped they become bitter. But God's work does not end with our first surrender. The diamond has been dug out of the ground but a good deal of cutting and grinding and polishing is necessary before it reaches its potential.

Acts 7:23 says Moses was forty years old when he rebelled and went into exile. Exodus says he was eighty when he returned to challenge the reigning Pharaoh. God's timetable sometimes appals us just as his methods sometimes amaze us. We are in a hurry – God is not! He has more to do than we think, before we are ready and the time is ripe. The cause of Moses' exile tells us something of his character and expectations:

One day after Moses had grown up, he went out to where his own people went and watched them at their hard labour. He saw an Egyptian beating a Hebrew, one of his own people. Glancing this way and that and seeing no one, he killed the Egyptian and hid him in the sand. (Ex 2:11–12.)

A born leader, young, strong and self-reliant, he was well placed to help the people of God and he knew it. Clearly, he was wondering how he could change the lot of his own people. Yet Moses needed to learn a lesson God would teach another leader, centuries later saying: 'Not by might nor by power but by my Spirit; says the Lord' (Zech 4:6). Moses had to learn to be a servant not a master, a prophet not a prince, the friend of God not of Pharaoh. And so God stripped him of his advantages and began his apprenticeship in spiritual leadership; an apprenticeship that was to last *another* forty years! Somebody has said, 'Moses spent his first forty years becoming a somebody, then his second forty years becoming a nobody and then God could use him.' But that long apprenticeship took the proud princeling and made him the humblest man on the earth (Num 12:3). And it was an apprenticeship in *faith*. Faith took him to Midian and faith kept him in Midian for forty years. But what a test of any person's vision and calling in God! It is hard to hold a vision for ten years let alone forty.

I can imagine Moses enjoying the first six months of healthy living away from the palace. I can imagine him even waiting for a year or two before contemplating a return. I can imagine him after a while saying, 'Well, Lord, let's get on with it, I've been here long enough.' Silence. No permission to go. Moses must wait. After ten years I can imagine him getting rather edgy with God ('I really am ready now Lord. I realise that I still wasn't ready after only a year or two – but it's now been ten')! And then as fifteen years became twenty and twenty became thirty and thirty became forty I can only see dreams in pieces, naive self-confidence drained away to the last drop, a steady, devout worshipper, humble, reliant, with no 'connections' in high places now except God! Moses is ready for his burning bush.

You may want to serve God significantly in your generation. Don't ask *where* does God need me, ask *how* does God need me. It is not your talent, your education or your connections God needs so much as your humility and love, your devotion to him and your reliance upon him. Let faith make its choice for God but let it be for God at all costs and for God anywhere.

13

FAITH TAKING SHELTER IN GOD (ISRAEL AND THE PASSOVER LAMB)

'*By faith he kept the Passover and the sprinkling of blood, so that the destroyer of the firstborn would not touch the firstborn of Israel*' (Heb 11:28).

When God enters a situation the first result sometimes is that things get worse! So it was when God came with Moses to liberate the Hebrews from Egypt. Moses and Aaron began by meeting the elders of the Israelites and telling them 'everything the Lord had said to Moses' at the burning bush and performing before the people the signs that had been given there (Ex 4:29–30). The result was that hope was born amidst a hopeless people, the log-jam of centuries was broken as they 'heard that the Lord was concerned about them' and they 'bowed down and worshipped' (Ex 4:31). It was the birth of hope – and it was also the beginning of fresh troubles (Ex 5:7–8, 14, 20–1).

Here begins the greatest advance in Israel's Old Testament history. God had come at last to do battle with Pharaoh and to liberate his people. After centuries of silence and seeming inactivity God is doing a new thing in the world. Yet in the event his 'new' work is not totally other than his everyday work. He does not call angels out of the skies (except one – as the climax of the plagues!); instead he calls his unnoticed battalions in nature: tiny bacteria and plankton in water, insects in the air, wind and hail, disease and darkness – and not an angel in sight!

Nearly all the wonders in these chapters can be filleted

of wonder by critics who cannot even be amazed at God. For the miracles are miracles not so much in the essence of what occurs as in the timing and the intensity of the plagues. Most of the plagues themselves are natural: what is supernatural and wonderful is the power which marshalls them and the purpose which guides them. To say they can nearly all be 'explained' scientifically is to miss the point. The point is, as Donald Bridge puts it:

> By God's intervention, at God's appointed time and by God's outstretched arm, a world dictator was confronted, a powerful false religion was humiliated, thousands of people were rescued from a hopeless situation and a rabble of slaves was transformed into the beginnings of a nation for God.[1]

The disgrace of the gods

In this entire series of events Jahweh of Israel makes a mockery of the 'gods' of Egypt: 'And the Egyptians will know that I am the Lord' (Ex 7:5). The Egyptians recognised some eighty gods at this time. Many of them are directly affected in their reputation and status by the plagues including *Hapi*, god of the Nile; *Hekht*, controller of frogs (with her crocodiles); *Egypt* itself whose sacred soil is polluted when her dust becomes 'alive' with gnats and hateful; *the scarab beetle*, symbol of royalty and a god overborn in the plague of flies; *the sacred bulls* felled by the plague which killed all the livestock; and the darkness that defeats '*Amen Ra*' the sun god, Pharaoh's supposed father. Even the priests are made impotent and ridiculous by a plague of boils! They are all, devotees and deities alike, helpless and dishonoured before the one God of heaven and earth.

A constantly recurring theme in these chapters in Exodus, along with that of the plagues, is the hardening of Pharaoh's heart which is referred to nineteen times in Exodus alone. It is a central feature in the build-up of tension in the narrative. The Nile turned to blood yet

Pharaoh 'did not take this to heart'. The land crawled with frogs. Pharaoh relented. Then 'he hardened his heart'. The air filled with swarms of insects and flies 'but Pharaoh's heart was hard', 'and would not let the people go'. Livestock and men were smitten 'yet his heart was unyielding' and in wrath Jahweh himself sealed his doom and hardened his heart to the end.

And so we come to chapter 11 with the reader as well as all Egypt on tenterhooks. Moses enters Pharaoh's presence with his final ultimatum and leaves hot with the indignation of God (Ex 11:4–11). All the signs and wonders, decisive and fearful as they were, did no good to Pharaoh. Why? Because they were not received with humble faith. In Scripture signs and wonders never make faith unnecessary or unimportant. Indeed they only 'work' for faith, that is they only profit when faith grasps their significance. As Donald Bridge observes 'There is always another possible explanation if you want to have one.'[2] As Christ's miracles did the Pharisees no good, so Moses' miracles did Pharaoh no good. Even though many of Jesus' miracles were greater, yet 'Christ could produce no credential so conclusive but that the Jews would demand one more conclusive sign still' (MacGregor).[3] So Pharaoh was never *quite* convinced.

Then we come to the greatest sign of all – the death of the first-born of Egypt. It will break Pharaoh's resolve, though as we shall see it will not make him another man: he is a vessel fitted for destruction (Rom 9:16–24) because of his incorrigible pride and rebellion. But it is not so much the tenth plague of Egypt as such that I am concerned with so much as the 'passing over' of Israel, the 'Passover' as it is called.

God is dangerous!

The most important and fundamental lesson which God taught Israel about himself in her early history was that God is holy and to sinners that holiness can be dangerous! This lesson confronts us here and in the entire book of

Leviticus with its sacrifices and sin-offerings. It teaches us that by nature we are sinners, unholy and corrupt before him and can only survive his judgement if our sin is dealt with. This was a lesson which had been impressed upon Moses and his wife in another connection a little earlier (Ex 4:24–6). The Old Testament scholar, Gordon Wenham, in his commentary on Leviticus, tells us that a basic principle which underlies the whole book is that 'the unclean and the holy are two states which must never come into contact with each other'.[4] If they do the result is disastrous and results in death. However, sacrifice by cleansing the unclean makes such contact possible. The holy God can then meet with sinful man. 'Peace with God,' writes Gordon Wenham, 'is the goal of sacrifice.'[5] We do read in Exodus 11:7 that God made a great distinction between Egypt and Israel but this was because of God's free and sovereign choice, his undeserved and faithful love, not because of merit or worthiness in Israel itself (Deut 7:6–8) as we can see from the nation's subsequent fickleness.

Hence, Israel must learn that it too cannot bear the approach of God! It is not clean and therefore is not safe. When the angel of death comes it is not only the first-born of Egypt who are in danger! But God gives the Israelites protection, he hides them 'under the blood' of the Passover lamb (Ex 12:22–3). He has given the blood to make atonement for the sin that forfeits life (see Lev 17:11). Israel is being *redeemed* from Egypt: at a price.

Christ our Passover Lamb

Our Lord Jesus linked himself to this whole Old Testament event when he celebrated the Passover, for the last time on earth, with his disciples (Mt 26:17–30; Mk 14:12–26; Lk 22:7–38).

Jesus reinterpreted and refocused the Passover meal. At two main points he made it the visible commemoration of his own sacrificial death for sin and the seal of his saving presence with his people. The Passover meal traditionally began with blessing and the sharing of the first cup of wine. Then the food was brought and in response to the eldest son's question 'Why was this night different from all other nights?', the father would recount the biblical story of the deliverance from Egypt. There would follow the sharing of the second cup. After that the unleavened bread would be passed around in silence and each participant would eat it with bitter herbs and stewed fruit.

But Jesus, as he distributed the unleavened bread, broke the silence, contrary to paschal custom, and interpreted the bread in terms of his own person saying, 'This is my body given for you; do this in remembrance of me' (Lk 22:19).

After they had eaten the roasted lamb of the Passover, the third cup of wine mixed with water was passed around. This third cup was called 'the cup of redemption' and it was of this cup that our Lord spoke when he said, focusing its significance on his own sacrificial death: 'This [cup] is my blood of the [new] covenant which is poured out for many' (Mk 14:24).

The traditional fourth cup of the Passover meal, 'the cup of consummation' Jesus refused to drink until the day of his second coming at the restitution of all things in the kingdom of God (Lk 22:18). So the Jewish Passover became the Christian 'Lord's Supper'. The Apostle Paul directly relates the Old Testament event with Christ's greater work when he tells the Corinthians: 'Christ our Passover lamb has been sacrificed', and urges them to live accordingly, facing the new future and abandoning the old ways (1 Cor 5:7), clearing out the old leaven of sin (cf. Ex 12:15). The Apostle Peter would also have had this event and the sacrifices of Leviticus in mind when he wrote: 'For you know that it was not with perishable things such as silver or gold that you were redeemed ... but with the precious blood of Christ, a lamb without blemish or defect' (1 Pet 1:18–19; cf. Ex 12:5; Lev 1:3–4). The New Testament is, in fact, permeated with the language and concept of atoning sacrifice in reference to Christ's work as Redeemer and Saviour. It is his wrath-bearing death, signified by his blood which is the hope and help of the world, the one covering for sin which saves us from the destructive judgement of a holy God (Rom 3:25–6; Gal 3:13; Heb 9:22,28 ;10:8–14). Only because of Christ crucified does the angel of death pass over us!

Let us keep the festival

Moses believed God not only for judgement on the oppressors, the Egyptians, but for mercy on the Israelites. 'Let us keep the festival' too says Paul, but this time in reference to a greater act of redemption. Here we learn that faith is confidence in the mercy, grace and love of God. It lays hold not only on his existence and power but also on his mercy and grace. John Calvin made this a part of his definition of faith in a famous statement. He wrote:

> Now we shall possess a right definition of faith if we call it *a firm and certain knowledge of God's benevolence toward us* founded upon the truth of the freely given promise in Christ, both revealed to our minds and sealed upon our hearts through the Holy Spirit.[6]

This conviction issues in trust, simple reliance upon the love of God in Christ; and such a reliance that puts its full weight upon this God and that love. Faith sees the faithfulness of God and rests on it and rejoices in it.

Some Christians, alas, scarcely know what it is to keep the festival. They go their whole lives through hardly daring to hope that on the day of judgement it will be well with them. They need to realise that for us the day of judgement has in one crucial respect already taken place. The Lamb of God has taken away our sin by bearing the punishment of sin in our place. If we have turned to him in repentance and faith then the blood of the Lamb is on our door posts too – however unworthy we may be within, and we can say:

112

No condemnation now I dread,
Jesus and all in Him is mine.[7]

For us the first words of prayer are not 'forgive us our trespasses' but 'Our Father in heaven', and for us the key note of our new life is not fearful hope but joyful festival. Such freedom and privilege calls for life-long gratitude, lives of serious consecration to God, lives which seek to honour him with holiness and a real hatred of sin: 'Therefore let us keep the Festival, not with the old yeast, the yeast of malice and wickedness, but with bread without yeast, the bread of sincerity and truth' (1 Cor 5:8).

If we have left Egypt let us be sure to leave the ways of Egypt too. We owe no allegiance to Pharaoh; he has no power over us now (Rom 6:16–22). We follow a different ruler – not Moses but Jesus, who rescues us from the coming wrath (1 Thess 1:10).

...in the last words of prayer, are not written words, but Leaves of prayer. Father in heaven, and these flowers fresh blooming of our life in their sweet hope and child period.

Such are love and privileges thus, for all they enjoyment or realization, as also to God everywhere to be born of him, will life gives us a realization of this. Promises is, to keep the Father, our with the God in all the past, or unjust and wickedness, one, will have, with useful meaning, bread in the truth, and little, God's love.

They have their moral laws a sure to laws, the wave of Egypt, too; the laws of allegiance to a church religions are passed over to now than a law. Z. We follow a laws and other — and loves he, Jesus Christ, teaches us from the coming world of Thess. 120.

14

FAITH PASSING THE POINT OF NO RETURN (ISRAEL AT THE RED SEA)

'*By faith the people passed through the Red Sea as on dry land; but when the Egyptians tried to do so, they were drowned*' (Heb 11:29).

Sometimes, I know, we are as much aware of our doubts as of our faith, as much aware of our sins as of our Saviour. We might, perhaps, find some comfort in the attribution of faith to the people who followed Moses. They followed complainingly and hesitantly, it is true, so that their faith was very imperfect, yet they stepped out in faith and trusted God to take them through the Sea of Reeds with all its instability and danger. Their faith took the decisive step. You may fear that your faith is not of good enough 'quality', but I ask you one thing – the essential thing: has it taken the decisive step, has it brought you to Christ for salvation? However badly you may think of your faith, do you now think well of your Saviour? That is the sign of a believer, a saved child of God, whose sin is covered and whose failure is made good in Christ Jesus 'who has become for us wisdom from God – that is our righteousness, holiness and redemption' (1 Cor 1:30).

Speculations and distractions

Of course the modern mind finds it fascinating to speculate on how the Israelites crossed the 'Red Sea' (literally, the Sea of Reeds, Ex 13:18) and what happened physically to make this possible. Some of the speculations are interesting but not more than that. Alan Cole in the Tyndale commentary on Exodus writes: 'If these were reedy salt marshes, with a soft bottom, connected with the main gulf (of which they would be the northerly extension) then a culmination of ebb tide and strong wind could dry them temporarily, long enough for a lightly-armed group to scamper across'[1] (Ex 14:22). He takes the phrase 'the waters being a wall' as a metaphor, not to be taken literally but indicating impassable lagoons to the right and left forcing the Egyptians to wait until the fiery cloud had moved away allowing the army to follow the route of the Israelites.

Another recent writer observes:

It is only in recent years that we have learned how unstable the areas of Suez and the Aegean Sea were in Moses' day ... it is only recently that a consensus of scholarly opinion has been reached that the two continents of Asia and Africa were in strong friction in early Old Testament times (the sliding plates theory) ... Where the Suez Canal now flows, in Moses' day there was a number of shallow, papyrus-filled lakes. A severe earthquake may well have heaved the Suez area several feet up, when the bottom of the gulf of Aquaba would subside to an equal extent. The waters of the shallow Sea of Reeds would then drain quietly away. Simultaneously there would be a tremendous wind caused by the quick elevation of the land surface. Then a second earthquake movement, again caused by the 'moving plate', could have swung the Suez area back to its original level or even lower, thus causing the sea from the Gulf of Suez to roar back into the Sea of Reeds. We must not forget that a tidal wave from the ocean, thirty-five feet high, overwhelmed the city of Tokyo at the great earthquake of 1923.[2]

All very interesting. Possibly instructive. Probably distracting! Our particular twentieth-century scientific 'mind set' is trained to ask 'how' rather than 'why', but in this matter 'why' is the more important question and to it Scripture gives three answers.

Matchless power

First: *God did this to glorify himself among the heathen.* Again and again this explanation is given:

> I will gain glory for myself through Pharaoh and all his army, and the Egyptians will know that I am the Lord. (Ex 14:4; cf. Ex 14:17–18.) The nations will cheer and tremble; anguish will grip the people of Philistia. The chiefs of Moab will be terrified, the leaders of Moab will be seized with trembling, the people of Canaan will melt away. (Ex 15:14–15.)
> It was news of this that helped to convince Rahab of the supremacy and truth of Israel's God (Josh 2:10), that helped the conquest of Canaan itself (Josh 2:11) and that led in part to the surrender and survival (by a ruse) of one entire people-group, the Gibeonites (Josh 9:9f). The demonstration of God's power over the armies of Egypt at the Red Sea is given a vivid touch in Exodus 14:27 – 'and the Lord swept them into the sea'. Knight notes that 'the verb actually means that he "flicked them away", shook them off as a man shakes fleas out of his bed clothes.'[3]

Those who refuse to be changed by God's love will one day be awed by his power. Whether or not they see them as they should, certain events in life, some of them on an international scene, bring home forcefully the power of God and the weakness of man, the eternity of God and the temporality of our empires and civilisations. We have seen, in our century, Communism rise to dominate one half of the world and to threaten the other half; yet we have also seen it crumble and fall away, having rotted from within and collapsed under its own weight. The ideology of Lenin and the armies of Stalin appeared to dwarf and threatened to crush the Church of God; but when the time was ripe 'he flicked them into the sea' and a wide-open door for the gospel appeared in Russia and Eastern Europe.

> So be it Lord! Thy throne shall never,
> Like earth's proud empires pass away;
> Thy kingdom stands and grows for ever
> Till all Thy creatures own thy sway.

Of course, it takes more than the failure of their systems to convince people of God's truth, but when arrogant dictatorships fall and aggressive ideologies fail, when fashionable trends and philosophies become outworn and discarded, when arrogant lifestyles and hedonisms end in sickness, disease and death, then confidence is shaken, questions are asked and minds are opened to new possibilities in new generations. People begin to say, 'Where did we go wrong?' and, 'Is there not a better way?' At such times the people of God need to speak up and give the reason for the hope they have (1 Pet 3:15).

Unfailing love

Second, God says he led Israel through the Sea and showed his power over Pharaoh's army at the Red Sea *to assure his people of his unfailing love*. After the event they could sing:

> I will sing to the Lord, for he is highly exalted. The horse and its rider he has hurled into the sea. The Lord is my strength and my song; he has become salvation. He is my God and I will praise him my father's God, and I will exalt him ... In your unfailing love you will lead the people you have redeemed. In your strength you will guide them to your holy dwelling. (Ex 15:1–2, 13.)

Thereafter, throughout their Old Testament history, the 'exodus' the 'going out', from Egypt was celebrated in their festivals and recalled in their songs. It was not only an exhibition of Jahweh's power but a demonstration of his love. By it Israel was visibly released from bondage and brought into freedom. It was the great redemptive act of God in their history: the type and model of all salvation.

We all need to know that God's love is an unfailing power as well as a generous attitude. We can appreciate that love quite easily on a Sunday, gathered together with other believers in worship, giving voice to the confession of a common faith and in a believing atmosphere where God's word is preached. Yet we must also rely on that love in the world outside and in the week that follows, when Pharaoh seems to have the power and when a whole army of pressures, fears, disappointments and perhaps dangers are bearing down on us. We need to hear the 'I will be with you' as we pray before work each morning; and when the world drowns out the whisper of the Spirit with its noise, and exposes our vulnerabilities with its bullying we need to know that the promise stands rock sure: 'Fear not, for I have redeemed you; I have summoned you by name; you are mine. When you pass through the waters I will be with you' (Is 43:1–2).

Trembling faith

Israel did not always trust the promises or remember the histories or live by faith. This very generation, the generation of the wilderness, would prove to be a tragic warning to future generations that faith is not just an initial act but a continuing lifestyle of dependance and obedience. It is strange that the writer of Hebrews should use Israel in his generation as an example of faith (he is, after all, under no illusions about them as we see from Hebrews chapter 3!). Indeed this crossing of the Red Sea at the command of Moses is the *only* act of faith ever recorded of this generation. Thereafter, their wilderness journeyings were a sad saga of instability, discontent and downright rebellion – quite the opposite of faith in fact. Yet here at least they act in such a way as to illustrate faith's commitment:

119

'By faith the people passed through the Red Sea as on dry land.'

Israel, after centuries of growing demoralisation, after suspicion, uncertainty and even resentment (Ex 4:8–9; 14:10–12) finally threw in their lot with Moses (Ex 14:13–22). *They passed the point of no return.* They identified with Moses; to use Paul's vivid metaphor – 'They were all baptised into Moses in the cloud and in the sea' (1 Cor 10:2). The discouraged readers of 'Hebrews' have also been baptised – not into Moses but into Christ. They have taken part in a far greater event than the redemption from Egypt; they have become the beneficiaries of a 'once-for-all' atonement and an eternal priesthood (Heb 8–10). How foolish and unnecessary to pine for the old covenant when they are partakers of the new covenant. Let them not repeat the failure as well as the initial success of Israel's faith.

Throughout Hebrews the most solemn warnings against turning back recur so that even faith learns to fear and to 'make its calling or election sure' (e.g. Heb 2:1, 3;3:7–19; 4:1–3; 6:4–12; 10:26–31, 35). Those warnings have always been read by Christians since, as they must have been by the letter's recipients then, with a degree of trepidation. Even if the final perserverance in faith and salvation of an elect child of God, justified in Christ, is certain (Jn 10:27–30; Rom 8: 28–30), such warnings and the fear they invoke may well be one of the means to *keep* them from the impossible (rather as you might say to a child, 'If you touch that hot fire you will be burned!') with the result that what is hypothetically spoken of never happens. Many have taken John Owen's position that the people envisaged in Hebrews 6:4–8 who 'fall away' into final condemnation were, like Judas, false converts, people who were never truly regenerate. More recently some have argued for a third category of believers who are saved (cf. 1 Cor 3:10–15) but who have spoiled their lives, ruined their witness, and will 'die in the desert' – a disappointment to God and a warning to man!

John Owen says the faith mentioned here in Hebrews

11:29 is the true faith of those who were not among the unbelievers who perished in the wilderness because of their sins.[4] There were, he says, true believers caught up, inevitably, in the judgement of God upon their generation. On this occasion, as Calvin puts it, the faith of the few saved the many.[5]

Irrevocable decision

Whichever view we take, the warnings to the readers of Hebrews are warnings to us all. There are times in our own lives when we who have become Christians can tire of the demands of our journey and hanker for the old life.

When you are tempted to 'go back', say: '*I have passed the point of no return*', 'I have been baptised into Christ', 'I am no longer my own', 'I have been bought with a price' (1 Cor 6:19–20; Gal 2:20). 'I belong to Christ my Lord – all other options are closed!'

There are times in life when we seem to be between Pharaoh's army and the Red Sea, 'between a rock and a hard place,' and nothing that we do can meet or match the occasion. At such times we may feel our faith to be very weak and the temptation very strong to complain against God as the Israelites did (Ex 14:11–12). Then we need to hear the voice, not of Moses but of God, saying, 'Do not be afraid' (for we often have more to fear from our fears than from our problems); 'Stand firm and you will see the deliverance the Lord will bring you today' (Ex 14:13). Sometimes we have to 'stand firm' for years and it is only from the longer perspective that we can see that God has fulfilled his good purposes for us. But whether God's 'today' is long or short, we can in such situations receive the promise and the strength and comfort of it by faith in a God who can always be trusted: 'The Lord will fight for you; you need only to be still' (Ex 14:14).

We may become disillusioned with fellow Christians or with ourselves, attracted to options and opportunities that are closed to us, weary with the constant struggle against 'the world, the flesh and the devil'!

Sometimes God's providence does lead us into impossible situations, dead-ends (Ex 14:1–4), but he is the God who can make a dead-end into a new beginning. 'Stand still' becomes 'move on' (Ex 14:15) through the impossible, over the insurmountable, beyond the limits of man and into the future of God.

15

FAITH AWARE OF GOD'S POWER (JOSHUA AND RAHAB)

'*By faith the walls of Jericho fell after the people had marched around them for seven days. By faith the prostitute Rahab because she welcomed the spies, was not killed with those who were disobedient*' (Heb 11:30–1).

For nearly forty years Israel wandered in the deserts between Egypt and Canaan, their promised land. It's an extraordinary story of divine faithfulness and human fickleness, the story of the failure of an entire generation. They had endured centuries of slavery in Egypt; God had shown his power and judgement upon the Egyptians in the ten plagues and had led them through the Red Sea in which the armies of Pharaoh had drowned. They were the most privileged generation in Israel's Old Testament history, and yet they perished in the wilderness because of unbelief (Heb 3:7–9).

All the miracles that followed them could not change the heart of a slave people that could have been and should have been the freedmen and women of God. They carried around their slave status in their hearts (Heb 3:10–12). They never fulfilled their potential or enjoyed their privilege. They had the name of God's chosen people but not the nature of God's true children. They entered into an external covenant; the spirit of the covenant never entered into them. Their one act of faith was in following Moses through the Red Sea – after that no other act of faith is recorded. Only in that one act are they a model for us (Heb 11:29). Even when they reached the borders of the promised land they were afraid to enter in and returned, for the lifetime of an entire generation, to the desert (Heb 3:18–19).

Here is a great warning to all nominal believers and to the children of Christians, who were raised in believing communities but who have no inner power of faith. Here is a warning too to those who take part in a great experience, perhaps a notable work of the Holy Spirit, who 'taste the powers of the age to come' but who do not build on it or keep faith with God and who soon 'fall in the wilderness' of the world's secular priorities. 'See to it, brothers, that none of you has a sinful, unbelieving heart that turns away from the living God. But encourage one another daily, as long as it is called Today, so that none of you may be hardened by sin's deceitfulness (Heb 3:12, 13).

A new beginning

And so we come to a new generation of Israelites: children who are determined not to make the same mistake as their parents. It is their calling to go up and possess the land God gave to Abraham. They too have a kind of Red Sea experience as the Jordan river is marvellously dammed up, allowing the whole army of priests and people to cross into their inheritance (Josh 3:14–17). Soon the challenging work of conquest will be given them, but first we have two significant chapters, Joshua 5 and 6, which in very different ways set the key note for the whole conquest.

In chapter 5 we have the mass circumcising of all the males of Israel. As a divine rebuke to the previous generation it had been denied them during the wilderness years. Now a new generation carries the mark of God upon their bodies. They are no longer an anonymous race of nomads; they are the consecrated heirs of God. They know who they are and what they must do.

You cannot do battle with life or for God in life without knowing who you are. Do you know who you are in relation to God? Are you sure of your sonship or daughterhood? Is the mark of God upon you? I don't mean a physical mark or an external ornament. Many have worn a cross around their neck who never yet carried one in their heart. But have you got the mark of God's ownership upon your inner and outer life in rebirth and public testimony? Are you *evidently* a Christian, are you *publicly* a Christian, have you stood forth, been baptised perhaps, so as to say to the whole world, or at least your world, 'I am no longer my own ... I belong to Christ' (Rom 10:9–11)?

A new strategy

As God's confirmed people Israel keeps the Passover and prepares to take Jericho. Jericho stood threatening and impregnable at the gateway to Canaan. There was no taking the country unless they took this particular city. But how are they to take it? Who will lead? Who else but Joshua and the New Model Army? But not in the first place! What is the strategy? God's strategy not man's. There is nothing wrong with *strategy* but there is something higher – *sovereignty*; the sovereignty of God almighty. Israel must learn that. And so we have an extraordinary test of faith and an unforgettable demonstration of God's control.

They are not allowed to attack the city. Soldiers and civilians are to walk around the city in solemn silent procession once each day for six days. How many of Joshua's troops must have itched for ropes and action! But they are not even allowed to raise their voices. Except for the weird sound of the rams' horns, they are to be a silent army waiting for Jahweh, their supreme commander, to work.

Once again the ground is prepared for a lesson constantly rehearsed in Scripture: '"Not by might nor by power but by my spirit," says the Lord' (Zech 4:6). And at the centre of significance: more than the army of Joshua, more than the hundreds of thousands who marched behind them, is the Ark of the Covenant which is carried by the priests in the midst of the host. *God* is circling the walls: the God who slew the first-born of Egypt, the God whose wrath burned out against Israel itself in the wilderness, the God whose judgement is as terrible as it is righteous and whose power none can resist. All the armies of the earth, ancient or modern, are scarcely the flicker of an image of that power which circled the walls of Jericho preparing to deal with the situation and open the way into the promised land.

On the seventh day they are to walk around it seven times. After the seventh time the rams' horns are to be silent until at Joshua's signal the army rends the air with the pent-up feelings of seven days. At that point Jericho's defences will collapse and the attack can begin from every direction.

Spiritual warfare

Hebrews 11:31 sees it all as a great act of faith on the part of Joshua and people. They shouted in faith before the walls fell (as Spurgeon once said, anyone could have shouted after the walls fell!). The great Puritan theologian, John Owen, comments: 'They triumphed by faith in the ruins of the walls [even] whilst they stood in full strength.'[1] We should remember, however, that they had a specific promise and revelation of the divine intervention. They did not 'name it and claim it' – God named it *then* they claimed it!

We too have Jerichos in the world around us: structures of evil built into our modern society, widespread unbelief and rampant materialism, credulous superstition and a despairing cynicism. Such Jerichos must fall if people are to be liberated. The walls are high, the city proud and independent. But God is still God and his power is undiminished. He has called us to war not against people but against the things that offend God and destroy human beings who were made to know him and to share his life. And so God begins to teach us the first lessons of spiritual warfare in the life of faith:

'The weapons we fight with are not the weapons of the world' (2 Cor 10:4).

'For our struggle is not against flesh and blood but

against ... the spiritual forces of evil in the heavenly realms' (Eph 6:12).

'Be strong in the Lord and in his mighty power. Put on the full armour of God so that you can take your stand against the devil's scheme' (Eph 6:10–11).

It is only as we use the weapons of God that we shall do the work of God and exercise 'divine power to demolish strongholds' (2 Cor 10:4). Those weapons Paul tells us plainly in Ephesians 6 are truth, righteousness, readiness, faith, salvation, the Word of God and prayer. It is with these things that we demolish 'every pretension that sets itself up against the knowledge of God' (2 Cor 10:5). It is by these things that we 'stand' and Satan 'flees' (Eph 6:14; Jas 4:7).

A lesson in prayer

Here surely we have a lesson in prayer too. In our Christian lives, in our attempts to witness to others and in our struggle for truth and justice in the workplace or in our society at large, we face our Jerichos, our walled cities of opposition, intransigent and aggressive; situations that defy us, events that stop us in our tracks, people who victimise us. What are we to do?

Often our first reaction is to meet force with force and aggression with open warfare or guile with more guile. We too can make a noise: so we batter at doors and blast walls and shout and threaten. Now sometimes in some situations some of these things are necessary, but almost always the first and most necessary response is simply to pray: to pray without noise, without fuss, without force. Our passions all call us to action but our faith calls us to prayer. We want to fight for the right but God wants us to *be* right with him first of all. We want to fight in our own strength but God wants us to fight in his. And so he calls us to pray, to plead, to intervene, to walk around the situation, to think about it and pray about it from every angle – and even then he sometimes says, 'Stand still and see the salvation of God.'

Of course by purely worldly standards nothing can be less appropriate, weaker or more pathetic. The situation demands strong action; what could be weaker than prayer? And indeed in terms of mechanical force nothing is weaker than prayer. Of itself prayer cannot turn the page of a book let alone knock down a wall. How can prayer change a mind or turn a situation round? How can prayer defeat cunning and the politics of life? How can prayer protect us, encourage us, lead us on?

The answer is that *prayer* can do none of these things but *God* to whom we pray can do all of these things. And he has told us to pray so that we always know that it is he who has done it and not the resources we can muster. Prayer is at once our greatest weakness and our greatest strength. We walk around Jericho again and again and nothing happens, but at the God-appointed moment, with a great shout, the walls come tumbling down, the opposition caves in, the malice of the enemy is defeated and the purposes and kingdom of God move on in unstoppable progress.

The walls of Jericho fell, the armies of Israel poured in, there was great carnage as the entire population was put to the sword and its city burned. I'm aware that that causes some people considerable problems these days – at any rate it often comes up as an objection to biblical religion – though why it should offend us more than others in a century which has bombed more cities and slain more populations than any in history I am not quite sure. We are actually no better than they and they at least had a divine mandate.

Israel's promised land was dotted with little city-states of the Canaanites (Amorites) and these were now under judgement. God had said to Abraham long before that he would wait until the sin of the Amorites reached its full measure (Gen 15:16). Clearly their's was a cruel culture and a depraved religion at this time and God pronounced a final judgement upon it. He is 'the compassionate and gracious God, slow to anger' yet he is also the righteous judge who 'does not leave the guilty unpunished' (Ex

34:7). There will come a time when he will call to account the entire population of the earth at the Second Coming of Christ. Then we shall witness a far more terrible and final judgement than this. So let us not sin with our easy criticisms and fashionable humanism: everything God does is right and God has a right to do anything he wills.

An unexpected convert

Meantime God is also in the business of rescuing people from a doomed world and a lost eternity. Rahab saved from Jericho is a memorable example. But we should notice that she was saved *in* Jericho before she was saved *from* Jericho. She is a striking example of faith where you would not expect to find faith (Josh 2:1–21).

I know that at this stage her faith was mixed. There were elements in it that are not to be copied. She lied like a trooper (plenty of experience I daresay!) to protect the spies but it could be argued that the authorities in Jericho had forfeited the right to truth at this stage. Still, in the New Testament she is recommended for her faith not her lie. A lie is in and of itself an evil thing. It belongs to chaos and the world of the fall. What trouble it has brought into the world of human affairs since Eden! Truth is precious to God for God is truth; the lie is essentially contrary to his nature and contradicts his reality. Yet in this fallen world there are times when to tell the truth can lead to a greater wrong than to conceal or even distort it. There are times when wickedness forfeits the right to truth and to deceive the enemies of goodness and justice becomes a lesser evil.

Here however, Rahab's faith dominates the picture and inspires us all. Rahab was denied every desirable means of spiritual help. She had no church, no Bible, no background of devout believers. Indeed she had been (perhaps earlier in life) a prostitute and now kept an inn built into the city wall. She kept an inn, not a convent! She would have heard plenty of news there of course from travellers and merchants and others. And the most pressing and disturbing news for weeks would surely have been the invasion of the land by the Israelites under Joshua their captain.

As people spoke of this people and their God, of the Red Sea deliverance a generation before, and the defeat of Pharaoh's entire army; as news came through of the defeat of the kings of the Amorites East of the Jordan (Josh 2:8–10) and of the miraculous crossing of the Jordan into Canaan, Rahab had begun to think of the God who was leading, protecting and championing this nation. She used every scrap of information she had and when the time came she knew whose side she wanted to be on. Her words to the spies are her confession of faith: 'The Lord your God is God in heaven above and on the earth below' (Josh 2:10).

She was the youngest, weakest believer that ever was. Yet she was challenged to put her faith to work: and as she did so her faith grew and also her significance in the ongoing work of God. We often think of learning from the heroic achievements of mature and prominent believers, but there are lessons to be learned from immature and very new believers too! Look at Rahab. She went against her whole background and culture and upbringing for the true God. She resisted every contrary loyalty as a false loyalty. She rose above her family background and her former way of life and risked everything, even her life, for this God, the God of Israel, the true God of heaven and earth.

What a lesson some people give us in their earliest days of faith! So full of joy, so ready to witness, so revolutionary in life. 'They'll learn,' we sometimes say. Yes, but will *we*? Young converts may be God's 'refresher course' in Christian life for us. As for them: it may be the time when they will do some of the most decisive and effective and admirable things ever for their Lord. Jesus made it quite clear that he must come before all others, before family, before culture, before the claims of any other (Mt 10:37, 38). Perhaps for you too the greatest act of faith, the greatest victory you ever win will be in your early days as

130

a believer when God calls an infant faith to do a mighty act.

A place in the Son

Joshua honoured Rahab's faith and her trust (Josh 6:17, 22–25). She was preserved, together with her family, when the city was destroyed. Moreover she was taken in to live among the Israelites (Josh 6:25). Indeed, Jewish tradition has it that she married Joshua himself thereby becoming the ancestress of priests and prophets including Jeremiah and Huldah. But far more striking, the genealogy of Christ in Matthew (1:5) has Rahab not as the wife of Joshua but of Salmon the ancestor of King David, who in turn was the ancestor of Jesus. Thus God honoured a woman who demonstrated true faith (Jas 2:25) and whose name is enrolled with honour in the traditions of both testaments.

God's power is power that can not only pull down walls but raise up lives – from squalor to purity, from ignorance to faith and from Satan to God (1 Thess 1:9). Look for the Rahabs in some of your Jerichos: the elect of God in unlikely places (Acts 18:9–10). It may seem you are confronted on all sides by unbelief, by materialism, even by ruthlessness and contempt. Yet there may be a Rahab amid it all, listening to your witness, looking at your life, and wondering if your God could become their God.

16

FAITH TAKING
ITS OPPORTUNITY
(BARAK, DEBORAH AND JAEL)

'And what more shall I say? I do not have time to tell about Gideon, Barak, Samson, Jephthah, David, Samuel and the prophets . . . (Heb 11:32).

The book of Judges is not my favourite book. At times it is almost heartbreaking to read. Moses is gone, Joshua is gone and Israel takes a nosedive into religious and moral anarchy. The history of the book of Judges over a period of about two hundred and fifty years records a wearisome cycle of judgement and mercy, retribution and deliverance (Judg 2:10–19). The book itself tells of an incomplete conquest at the start (Judg 2:1–3) and of civil war at the end (Judg 20:21, 24, 31, 35, 46), and includes terrible accounts of apostasy, immorality and massacre.

Yet the book also contains accounts of good people, brave deeds and national repentance (or at least tribal repentance). God raises up charismatic figures (in all senses of the word) who rally the nation in times of defeat and recall them back to old faith and standards. Some of these great leaders are themselves flawed and reflect the times in which they lived. They were the judges after whom the book is named.

By the time of Deborah, Israel had been fragmented, disorganised and dishonoured for twenty years (Judg 4:2–3).

Israel was suffering under the oppression of the Canaanites (Judg 4:2f) and the land was in a state of near anarchy: the caravan-roads were in danger and traffic almost ceased; the cultivated lands were plundered; the fighting men in Israel were disarmed and neither shield nor spear could be found among forty thousand in Israel (Judg 5:6–8).[1] Then God raised up Deborah (Judg 4:4–5).

Deborah: faith challenging

When God chose a woman to lead Israel, he no doubt shocked a conservative and patriarchal society. Yet his choice must have been made very clear and her gifts must have been unmistakable. She did the job. For forty years she judged Israel and we read 'the land had rest from their enemies' (Judg 5:31).

Deborah saw and felt the tragedy of her time (Judg 5:6–7) but she did not subordinate God to the times. Like others after her she acknowledged that God was unchangeably holy and faithful and sovereign (cf. Hab 1:12–13). This was her starting point. In his own time he would act for his own great name. When he did act she was ready. When he spoke she heard and believed the call of God (Judg 4:6–7). Deborah was fully aware of the scale of the problem but she was not dominated by the problem; she was a woman dominated by God and so of all the people was free to help them in their hour of need. Though Deborah had seen the spiritual life of Israel sink very low, she felt the warm breath of God's spirit breathing new life into the nation and knew that a new day was dawning: the day of God's power.

Here was the faith that heard God's revelation and believed it and acted on it:

> She sent for Barak son of Abinoam from Kedesh and Naphtali and said to him, 'The Lord God of Israel commands you: "Go, take with you ten thousand men of Naphtali and Zebulun and lead the way to Mount Tabor. I will lead Sisera the commander of Jabin's army, with his chariots and his troops to the Kishon River and give him into your hands."' (Judg 4:6–7.)

Militarily it made no sense at all: Jabin's army had nine hundred Canaanite chariots of iron which were useless in the hills but irresistible on the plains yet the chariot-less Israelite soldiers were *to go down* to the river Kishon. The enemy would have all the advantages, the situation seemed impossible, the odds a thousand to one but Deborah was a spiritual heir of Joshua and she believed the promise of his dying speech to the leaders of Israel a generation before:

The Lord has driven out before you great and powerful nations; to this day no one has been able to withstand you. One of you routs a thousand, because the Lord your God fights for you, just as he promised. So be very careful to love the Lord your God. (Josh 23:9–11.)

That was precisely the calling and promise set before the Jewish believers of New Testament times to whom this letter was addressed. They were outnumbered and outlawed, regarded as traitors to their nation yet they were pioneers of a new day in the life of the world, a day which would bring light to the nations as the darkness was challenged and driven back:

But Paul and Barnabas spoke out even more boldly: 'It was necessary that the word of God should be spoken first to you. But since you reject it and do not consider yourselves worthy of eternal life, we will leave you and go to the Gentiles. For this is the commandment that the Lord has given us: "I have made you a light for the Gentiles, so that all the world may be saved."' When the Gentiles heard this, they were glad and praised the Lord's message; and those who had been chosen for eternal life became believers. (Acts 13:46–8.)

They all seemed so weak, so small, so pathetic in comparison with Caesar's legions, Rome's greatness and a world full of other and older religions. Yet today the gods are forgotten, the Roman Empire is history and Jesus Christ is known and loved by millions across the globe. True, there is still much ground to be claimed for him, but with Deborah's spirit and New-Testament faith we can do it.

The great missionary to China, Hudson Taylor, used to say that in doing God's work there were often three stages: impossible, difficult and done. We find it impossible when we consider the odds, the chariots of man; but we have a choice: we can either count the odds or the opportunities. In words made famous by John F. Kennedy a generation ago: 'Some people look at what is and ask "Why?" I look at what could be and ask "Why not?"' It is a characteristic of faith that seeing the invisible it challenges the visible, seeing what will be it seeks to change what is, moving towards the future it shapes the present.

Barak – faith faltering

'Behind every good man there is a good woman' runs the old saying. There is an unwritten history of the world – and it is the history of the ways in which women have influenced men. It has been recognised ('the hand that rocks the cradle rules the world') but it has not been written up. Countless lives have been shaped by the influence of a mother and a wife and many men have testified to the fact that they would not, could not, have been what they became or have done what they did without the influence and backing of the women in their lives. And Barak is among them. For Barak would never have been enrolled among the men of faith if it had not been for the influence of a woman of faith whose faith was stronger than his. Deborah was neither his mother nor his wife yet under the anointing of God she refashioned Barak in one day from a cautious leader with a mediocre faith into a decisive general who brought three tribes of Israel together and routed the armies of Sisera at Kishon.

Faith hesitating

Barak was not without faith, he too was a true Israelite, but faced with the enormous odds against them (the nine hundred chariots of iron were the equivalent to him of a squadron of B52s!) and calculating the risk to all his troops, his faith faltered. You and I might have thought that Barak's reply to Deborah when confronted with her call was very reasonable: 'Barak said to her, "If you go with me, I will go: but if you don't go with me, I won't go"' (Judg 4:8). Deborah however saw it in a different light. She was a recognised prophet (Judg 4:4) and she had given her call as from the Lord: 'The Lord, the God of Israel, commands you: "Go..."' (Judg 4:6).

Perhaps Barak thought that the presence of the prophetess in his battle, like the presence of the ark of the covenant in others, would be a greater guarantee of success. Perhaps he even thought that God at a distance might not be as effective as God close up! Deborah's response to his halfway faith was stern and uncompromising: '"Very well," Deborah said, "I will go with you. But because of the way you are going about this, the honour will not be yours, for the Lord will hand Sisera over to a woman"' (Judg 4:9–10).

The result was that Barak summoned ten thousand fighting men of Israel from the tribes of Zebulun and Naphtali and they went to the region of Mount Tabor and the Kishon River where Sisera met them with his formidable army and their nine hundred iron chariots: 'Then Deborah said to Barak, "Go! This is the day the Lord has given Sisera into your hands. Has not the Lord gone ahead of you?"' (Judg 4:14).

Faith engaging the enemy

What followed, and the complete and utter rout of Sisera's host is graphically portrayed in the Song of Deborah: 'O Lord when you went out ... the earth shook, the heavens poured, the clouds poured down water ... The river Kishon swept them away, the age-old river, the river Kishon. March on, my soul; be strong!' (Judg 5:4, 21).

Arthur Cundall has very convincingly captured the scene and indicates what happened. Pointing out that

137

Sisera would not have been so foolish as to deploy his chariots in the rainy season, he writes that:

> The words of Deborah's song suggest an unusual torrential downpour, possibly a thunderstorm, which came after the normal season of the latter rains in April and early May ... The ten thousand Israelites lightly armed and highly mobile, poured down into the valley and joined battle with a chariot force which was unable to manoeuvre on the softened ground. Escape, with the possibility of fighting under better conditions on another day was the only wise course ... But as they made their way in a general north-westerly direction, with the Israelites in hot pursuit, the valley narrowed, decreasing the space available for deployment. This caused chariot to jostle with chariot, churning up the surface of the ground and making it even more difficult for those in the rear of the panic-stricken army. Meanwhile the river would continue to rise as it was fed by innumerable small tributaries, rushing down from the surrounding hills ... The words of Deborah must have formed the epitaph of many, 'the river of Kishon swept them away'. 'Then the land had peace for forty years' (Judg 5:31).[2]

Faith overcoming doubt

I'm not altogether sure why the writer of Hebrews mentions Barak rather than Deborah in his list (after all he had just saluted Rahab), but I'm pretty sure that when he *referred* to Barak everyone would have *thought* of Deborah! It may be that Barak was specially useful for his purposes because all his readers would have known that Barak's faith had not been without its defect and doubt. His example therefore offers some particular encouragement (and even rebuke?) to wavering believers.

It is a well-known fact of life that the truly brave man or woman is not the one who knows no fear but rather the one who feels and faces their fear and yet presses on through danger towards goals set by a sense of righteousness, justice or compassion. The greatest courage involves the conquest of fear not the absence of fear.

So too the greatest faith involves not the absence of doubt but the refusal to let doubt paralyse us and the determination to press on in response to a truth we have seen, a call we have recognised, a vision we have been given. Doubt is only properly dealt with by faith developed in understanding *and* obedience. Passive intellectual cogitation is not enough. Faith must be put to *work* and *worship*: 'My teaching is not my own. It comes from him who sent me. If anyone chooses to do God's will, he will find out whether my teaching comes from God or whether I speak on my own' (Jn 7:16–17).

Faith's victory is not that it exists without doubts but that it is decisive over doubt. It understands and believes enough for *commitment* to Jesus Christ. Don't let your doubts crowd out your certainties. Your doubts may be real and great but they nowhere equal the massive certainties of God, Christ and salvation. It is the same with our ongoing Christian lives, too, even in hard times. Os Guiness reminds us in his book *Doubt: Faith in Two Minds*:

> We do not trust God because he guides us; we trust God and then are guided, which means that we can trust God even when we do not seem to be guided by him. Faith may be in the dark about guidance, but it is never in the dark about God. What God may be doing may be a mystery, but who God is is not.[3]

Jael: Faith deciding

Sisera himself survived the carnage of battle and fled towards Hazor in a state of shock and exhaustion. In the same area the nomadic group of the Kenites had settled and it is one of these, Jael the wife of Heber the Kenite, who sees the fleeing commander pass near her own tent and calls him in, offering safety and rest. Cundall observes: 'The offering and acceptance of hospitality in a nomad's tent was, traditionally, a guarantee of protection. Moreover any pursuer would hardly think to look in a woman's tent for a man, let alone a weary fugitive, for this would be a breach of etiquette.'[4] So Sisera, lulled into a false sense of security eats, drinks and lies down and sleeps, an exhausted man. And Jael is faced with her great though terrible opportunity.

I can see her sitting in the gloom of her tent, piecing together recent events, grasping the situation and suddenly realising that she is in an extraordinary and unique position. God has delivered into her hands the symbol of cruel oppression, the one man who can revive the fortunes of the Canaanites so that the monster lives again. Picture the exhausted figure in shock and sleep. Jael reaches for familiar instruments (the *women* were the expert tent-builders then). She holds the tent pin above his forehead, takes aim, and smites it home: the figure jerks; she smites it again: the figure convulses; again she strikes it deeper till it reaches the earth. The figure lies stretched out and lifeless. It was a terrible decision which called for a fearsome courage. But it was her supreme moment:

> There is a tide in the affairs of men
> Which, taken at the flood, leads on to fortune;
> Omitted, all the voyage of their life
> Is bound in shallows and in miseries.[5]

Now I have to tell you that Jael, the wife of Heber the Kenite has not had a good press: 'an act of treachery which cannot be condoned' says one, 'an unheard of breach of the sacred laws of eastern hospitality' says another, 'an act of callous efficiency' protests a third and, my favourite, from a Victorian dean (of great excellence I may say), 'we shrink instinctively from the blood-stained hand of Jael. She has overstepped the line between the feminine and the masculine'! However, when I consider the savagery of the Canaanites and the horrors of oppression I, very improperly no doubt, want to join Deborah in the congratulations of chapter 5 verses 24–7.

It is pretty grim stuff I know but so will the Judgement Day be and so is judgement in many of its forms. I rather think Jael belongs with those German officers who tried to blow up Hitler. At any rate I think no tears were shed for Sisera in Israel and even for the most sensitive traveller through the book of Judges the sound of his mother's lament would surely be drowned by the celebrations of Israelite women and children at the news of his death and his army's defeat. Deborah's song, an Old Testament magnificat, would have been the hymn in Israel on that day with its triumphant ending: 'So may all your enemies perish O Lord! But may they who love you be like the sun when it rises in its strength' (Judg 5:31).

17

FAITH LEARNING TO
FIGHT (GIDEON)

Our first meeting with Gideon does not impress. He is
'threshing wheat in a wine press to keep it from the
Midianites' whose marauding bands have reduced Israel
to poverty and disgrace. Suddenly a figure appears whom
he takes for a prophet and a conversation begins which
will change not only Gideon's life but Israel's fortunes for
a generation:

> When the angel of the Lord appeared to Gideon, he said,
> 'The Lord is with you, mighty warrior.' 'But sir,' Gideon
> replied, 'If the Lord is with us, why has all this happened
> to us? Where are all his wonders that our fathers told us
> about when they said, "Did not the Lord bring us up out
> of Egypt?" But now the Lord has abandoned us and put
> us into the hand of Midian.' The Lord turned to him and
> said, 'Go in the strength you have and save Israel out of
> Midian's hand. Am I not sending you?' (Judg 6:12–14.)

At this point in his life Gideon hardly seems a 'mighty
man of valour' as he threshes his pitiful harvest in the
hollow of the wine press. But these words, besides pointing to his potential as a leader, are prophetic: this is what
he will be because this is what God will make him.
Already the Spirit of the judges is working in him although
he does not realise it. Therefore he is to go in the strength
he has (Judg 6:14) and 'save Israel out of Midian's hand'.

What we are and can be

How many believers have empathised with Gideon's
speech in verse 13: 'Where are all his wonders that our

fathers told us about?' We look back on the Church's great times of revival or evangelism or missionary expansion with their great preachers and pioneers and evangelists and contrast those days with our own, especially in the West where the churches, even the more successful ones, make such a small impact on our society.

Yet the call comes to us in our day: Go in the strength you have.' 'The one who is in you is greater than the one who is in the world' (1 Jn 4:4); 'who is able to do immeasurably more than all we ask or imagine, according to his power that is at work within us' (Eph 3:20). In our world so many live without God, the tide of godless and often ruthless materialism has risen so high, huge bureaucracies and multinational corporations have become so complex, so lacking in a human face, so hard to change, that the Christian feels like Gideon: 'But, Lord, how can I save Israel?' (Judg 6:15).

The answer now is the same as the answer then: '*I will be with you*' (Judg 6:16). We shall find that the Midianites are not as strong as we think. People are suffering in the very systems they are desperately trying to ride. The possibilities in God are as great as they ever were; the Christian voice in society if sounded intelligently, consistently and faithfully can turn the tide of moral decay, family breakdown, ruthlessness in business practices and, above all, ignorance of God. In the days of the judges the Spirit of God fell on only one Gideon. In these New Testament days God has millions of Gideons (Acts 1:8; 2:38–9). The great need now is for Christians in society to 'go in the strength you have' and see what God will do with each day's going.

Gideon's apprenticeship and ours

In spite of his modest words to the angel – who is really the Lord himself (Judg 6:14, 22) – 'How can I save Israel? My clan is the weakest in Manasseh, and I am the least in my family' (Judg 6:15), it is clear that in fact Gideon's family are prominent and comparatively wealthy. Gideon himself has ten servants and his own establishment even though his father Joash is head of the family. It is here that Gideon's first test and challenge lies.

When God called Gideon to himself he called for an absolute and exclusive loyalty. In doing so he called him to renounce and oppose the false religion of his own family and village. More than that, because Israel belonged to the Lord, Gideon was given explicit authority and direction to demolish an important village shrine devoted to Baal, the god(s) of fertility and fruitful harvest, the property of his own father (Judg 6:24–6). He was further instructed to raise an altar to Jahweh in its place and on it to sacrifice one of his father's full-grown and most valuable bulls. We ought to realise the serious cost of that alone. Burning the family Volvo would be nothing to it! But to God that village shrine epitomised Israel's divided heart. Israel wanted the blessing of Jahweh *and* the Baals, but God will not tolerate two altars in Israel's life – or in yours and mine (Mt 6:24).

Jesus too called for such supreme loyalty and put himself in the place of God when he said to his followers, 'Whoever loves his father or mother more than me is not fit to be my disciple; whoever loves his son or daughter more than me is not fit to be my disciple' (Mt 10:37). We must never put our family or our country or our friends above God. We must never say, 'My family right or wrong,' or, 'My country right or wrong.' That attitude and resolution has nourished feuds between families and wars between nations. Jesus called for the supreme loyalty due to God alone and knew that that would set 'a man against his father, a daughter against her mother, a daughter-in-law against her mother-in-law; a man's enemies will be members of his own household' (Mt 10:35–6).

There is of course a positive side to this and also to our apprenticeship in God. They say charity begins at home but so do many other things including the Christian life. One of the earliest and hardest tasks of the life of faith is putting things right on the home front: saying openly to parents and brothers and sisters or wife or husband or children, 'I serve a new master now and my way of life is going to be different,' 'I've found God the greatest friend and the real meaning of life and I want you to know him too,' 'Jesus Christ has saved me and he can save you also.' It is never easy to make a new stand in an old situation; to stand for God and godliness where they know you so well; to rise, perhaps above fear as well as embarrassment: to have the conversation, to write the letter, to make the telephone call. It is likely to make you very nervous, to bring you on your knees, but Christ's soldiers fight best on their knees and you may be astonished at the responses you meet with in some of your family.

In those lawless days such an action was likely to cost Gideon his life and nearly did (Judg 6:30). Fortunately, to Gideon's father blood was thicker than water and he ingeniously saved his son from the mob (Judg 6:31). That itself may have been a sign to Gideon that God was with him in the work and would not abandon him, but what followed was an even greater sign. Remember that these 'judges' God raised up were men and women extraordinarily endowed with the Spirit of God. He gave them their insight and authority to judge in Israel, he raised respect for them in the hearts of the Israelites and he accompanied their call to arms with the exciting and drawing power of his Spirit. That is why we read that when the bedouin coalition next came up against the people, 'the Spirit of the Lord came upon Gideon' so that he sent messengers to summon the menfolk of the tributes to him and an astonishing thirty-two thousand gathered to defend their land in battle. Here was a 'sign and wonder' in itself, but Gideon wanted more proof that God was with him and would save Israel by his hands and so we have the fleece he put out and the tests he gave to God.

Fleeces and foolishness

He did it humbly and not arrogantly but it was not so much an act of faith as a confession of faith's weakness.

God had already commissioned Gideon (Judg 6:14) and equipped him. God had even given him several memorable signs (Judg 6:21, 31, 35). Yet here we have Gideon asking for more! However, God patiently and in grace acceded and gave Gideon the signs he asked for: the wet fleece when all around was dry and the dry fleece when all around was wet (Judg 6:36–40).

Gideon's 'fleece' has passed into the evangelical vocabulary. People talk about 'putting out a fleece' to find out if their intentions or initial actions are right before God. Now I know that 'guidance' is often a difficult matter in life-decisions where God's word is silent and his will unclear. We ask, 'Is this the right career, the right person, the right house, the right church for me?' Then we have to proceed carefully and prayerfully with good sense and a surrendered will. This is better than listening for a voice in the mystic silence or looking for a sign in the events of the day. There may be a voice or a sign and it may be of God, but the conviction which grows from a prayerful heart awake to all the facts and attentive to the counsel of mature and spiritual friends is likely to be a safer and truer way of finding out God's will for you in a situation. If we do this God will guide us, and if we make a wrong decision he is still sovereign and well able to encompass it in his plan for our lives, over-ruling it to good and turning us back to his prepared path.

I know of course that we must have an eye to Providence and the course of events in this matter of guidance. Sometimes God makes his will known in striking ways. However, asking God for 'signs' is a risky business. Satan can wet fleeces as well as God, and the twist and turn of events can sometimes produce 'encouragements' which turn into dead-ends. The best thing to do in such cases is to retreat as soon as possible back into open space and the alternative possibilities of life. I have never been able to understand people who put out fleeces years ago and have held God, ever since, to a promise he has not made, a purpose he never had and a dream he has no intention whatever of making a reality. This is not faith but delusion. It is perhaps well meant but foolish. It may, of course, be simply selfish and stubborn. Be careful with fleeces; they make good stories but poor arguments. Do not put God to the test; he is under no obligation to respond.

God however is very patient and good. He indulges Gideon, gives him his signs and leads him to:

Gideon's greatest hour

Chapter 7 opens with a sight that surely cheers us – thirty-two thousand Israelites rediscovering their identity as the people of God, recovering their national spirit and marking hopefully the turn of the tide. Admittedly there are one hundred and thirty-five thousand of the opposition (Judg 8:10), a bedouin coalition of Midianites and Amalekites and 'Ishmaelites', but with God's help a dedicated, determined, faithful army of thirty-two thousand can still win the day at odds of only four to one.

Then comes one of Gods surprises: 'There are too many, Gideon,' 'Yes Lord, one hundred and thirty-five thousand of them to only thirty-two thousand of us.' 'No Gideon, I mean there are too many of us!' There follows two tests to bring the numbers down. Gideon is told to 'encourage' those who 'tremble with fear' and cannot cope to go home – and twenty-two thousand avail themselves of the offer (Judg 7:2–3). Then the remaining ten thousand are reduced to only three hundred by a simple test of battle-readiness: the way they drank at a mountain stream (Judg 7:4–8). Of course I know that it made some sense militarily to get rid of the faint-hearted and of the easily-distracted too, but it made no sense *any* human way to face one hundred and thirty-five thousand with three hundred and look for a victory: a ratio of one Israelite farmer with little weaponry to four hundred and fifty well-armed and experienced desert warriors!

The lesson is one we have learned elsewhere: 'Not by might nor by power but by my Spirit says the Lord Almighty' (Zech 4:6). 'God chose the foolish things of the world to shame the wise; God chose the weak things of

148

the world to shame the strong ... so that no one may boast before him' (1 Cor 1:27–9). I like the words of a once-famous Victorian preacher, Joseph Parker of the City Temple:

> When did God ever complain of having too few people to work with? I have heard him say, 'Where two or three are gathered together in my name I am there.' I have heard him say, 'One shall chase one thousand and two shall put ten thousand to flight.' But I never heard him say, 'You must get more men or I cannot do this work; you must increase the human forces, or the divine energy will not be equal to the occasion.'

God has always been more concerned with quality than quantity, more pleased with a few hearts fully surrendered than many hearts divided between him and the world. The Church has constantly to be taught this lesson. We are too easily impressed by numbers. John White writing with Ken Blue on church discipline warns us that 'the Church's growth is largely a cancerous growth and we do not even know it'.[1] We are always asking God to increase the Church. Ought we not to be asking him to refine it? Throughout Church history there has been a correlation between church discipline and healthy church growth. Many churches would be twice as effective if they were half the size.

We say 'Man's extremity is God's opportunity.' Gideon however is very shocked and deeply fearful (Judg 7:10) – and who can be surprised? So God helps Gideon with yet another sign. He sends him and his servant, Purah, on a reconnaissance to the outskirts of the camp where they overhear, by divine appointment, a Midianite recounting to his fellow-soldier a dream of the destruction of the Midianite army by the weakest of means (Judg 7:13–14). I like the observation of C.H. Spurgeon here:

> Now observe, first, the providence of God that this man should have dreamed just then, and that this man should

have dreamed that particular dream. God is as divine in the small as in the stupendous, as glorious in the dream of a soldier as in the flight of a seraph ... Dreamland is chaos, but the hand of the God of order is here. What strange romantic things our dreams are! – fragments of this and broken pieces of the other, strangely joined together in absurd fashion. Yet observe that God holds the brain of this sleeping Arab in his hand and impresses it as he pleases ... Oh believe it, God is not asleep when we are asleep; God is not dreaming when we are.[2]

A worshipping, joyous Gideon returns to his waiting three hundred and following a carefully prepared plan arms them with the only human weapons which can hope to win the day – panic! In the dead of night the little force divides into three companies which creep up on the sleeping army: rams'-horn trumpets in one hand, and their jars hiding burning torches in the other. At the given moment the three companies together smash the jars, wave the torches and furiously blow the trumpets again and again. The waking Midianites and Amalekites and others rush out confused and convinced they are being invaded or perhaps betrayed each by the other tribes. In the dark they strike out at each other and increase the panic and the violence. Their camels stampede increasing the turmoil and injury. Gideon's army does next to nothing: the enemy do it all! Soon the field is littered with bodies and discarded weapons and it is left to the three hundred (and their former fellow-soldiers and others from the tribe of Ephraim) to pursue the remnant of the invading army and finish the task (Judg 7:23–4). Midian is defeated. Israel is free. Gideon is the deliverer and the Lord is God.

It's the opposition which is outnumbered!

I do not have time to tell, says the writer of Hebrews 11, all I could tell of Gideon and the others. But because he is writing to Hebrews who know their Old Testament well, you can be sure that the mention of Gideon would recall for them the story of the three hundred against the one hundred and thirty-five thousand. And no doubt these Hebrew Christians, these Jews for Jesus, feel they are very much like that three hundred. They too are hugely outnumbered by the Israelites of Judea, Galilee and the dispersion. How many serve the God of their fathers (the true God!); how few follow Jesus of Nazareth. How old is the old faith; how new is the new Way. How splendid are the histories of the nation Israel; how contemptible by comparison are the beginnings of Christianity.

These vulnerable Jewish Christians, so ostracised in their communities, often persecuted and suffering, need to hear that what was splendid about Israel's past was not the outward glories or the apparent strength but *faith* which made the difference and marked the true people of God. And that faith now lives in them, focused more clearly than ever, because focused on Jesus, the Son of God, the way, the truth and the life. Moreover *he* has by his death and resurrection won the great and decisive battle. Now that the final outcome is determined they can hold their ground and more, they can be 'more than conquerors' through him that loved them (Rom 8:37), bringing the good news to fellow-countrymen who are willing to hear and to all people that the Messiah has come, the Son of God to set us free.

As Gideon's story inspired them so it can inspire us. We too face the world feeling outnumbered. We see against us a great coalition of secular humanists, rival religions, ruthless business interests and godless materialism. We often see these as a united and strong force, full of successful people dismissive of Christ's claims and confident in their own philosophy. The truth however is very different. The coalition is divided against itself and its individuals are often desperately insecure and uncertain. Competing forces pull them or threaten or crush them; the world is both their friend and their enemy. They have their dreams – and their nightmares. Into their world can roll sickness or bereavement and suddenly the fragile tent collapses, the hopes fade, the gains of life turn to ashes and there is no one to help.

Better to be with God's three hundred than the Midianites' one hundred and thirty-five thousand, 'for if God is for us who can be against us?' (Rom 8:31). The future lies with us and all the coalitions of earth and hell cannot keep us from that future or separate us from the love of God that is in Christ Jesus our Lord.

It is not the people of God, but the opposition which is outnumbered:

> After this I looked and there before me was a great multitude that no-one could count, from every nation, tribe, people and language, standing before the throne and in front of the Lamb ... And they cried out in a loud voice: 'Salvation belongs to our God, who sits on the throne, and to the Lamb' (Rev 7:9, 10).

18

FAITH RISING ABOVE REJECTION (JEPHTHAH)

I have to confess to having a tender spot for this man. His life began and ended in tragedy, yet in his way he was faithful against all the odds. He was the son of an Israelite and a prostitute – illegitimate, despised, dispossessed, driven out of his home and family by his own brothers (Judg 11:1–3). You can imagine the memories, the scars, the fantasies and frustrations. He was the brightest of them all. Yet his half-brothers threw him out and denied him any share of his inheritance. But God chose this man above all others to be a judge of Israel and a figure in the honours list of Hebrews 11.

Unexpected choice

First of all, here is a lesson in God's choice. Once again we are led to familiar words of Paul; let us hear them this time in the *Good News Bible*:

Now remember what you were, my brothers, when God called you. From the human point of view not many were wise or powerful or of high social standing. God purposely chose what the world considers weak in order to shame the powerful. He chose what the world looks down on and despises, and thinks is nothing, in order to destroy what the world thinks is important. This means that no one can boast in God's presence. (1 Cor 1:26–29.)

'God chose the lowly things of this world and the despised things and the things that are not' (NIV) and no one was more despised than Jephthah. Never was there among the things that 'are not' in human valuation anything as little considered as the developing foetus that grew in the womb of the unnamed prostitute, fathered by Gilead and wanted by no one. Gilead took the baby, I know, but what a perpetual reminder of his sin this growing child was, and as the boy grew towards manhood what a threat he became to the inheritance – or rather to the inheriting sons who drove him away.

Yet God was in that chain of events – even in the first link of it, preserving the conception, protecting the foetus and providing a home for the baby. This child too would be able to say in later years, 'All the days ordained for me were written in your book before one of them came to be' (Ps 139:16). For God would bring Israel's next deliverer from the ranks of the illegitimate and the rejected, and the insiders would be saved by an outsider who came in out of the cold at the entreaty of the very people who had rejected him (Judg 11:4–11). Here surely if ever we have one is a lesson in God's choice and one which must have comforted those Christians who received the letter to the Hebrews, some of whom may also have been rejected and cast out from their families.

Inalienable dignity

Second, *here is a lesson in human freedom and dignity* when God offers 'a better way' than defeat, self-pity and despair. It is a dehumanising 'humanism' which regards or treats people merely the *products* of something: whether heredity, environment, social or economic factors. We should weigh these factors carefully but never make the human person a mere result, the 'inevitable' product of external forces. Nothing can alter the facts of your past. But what is more decisive is your attitude to your past and your response to it.

God can free you from the tyranny of sin and its effects in your life (even other people's sin!). God can make a prize out of a reject, a child out of an outcast! Do you sometimes feel an outsider? Are there circles of influence and privilege which always keep you on the margins even though they have no more, and perhaps less, gifts, abilities, or potential for good in the situation than you? Look to God above and beyond the situation; look hard and long. Seek his companionship and approval above all. Aim to please him and you will never find him careless of your efforts or contemptuous of your achievements. If you invest all your hopes in people you will inevitably be disappointed somewhere along the way. If you invest in God you will never lose one single prayer or longing or act of faith and love; all will be treasured and great will be the day of approval when he says, 'Well done, good and faithful follower.'

Learn too from Jephthah's treatment at the hand of his brothers not to overlook and never to despise anyone around you who may not have your advantages, your kind of background, your beginnings, your abilities. They may be very dear to God, their struggles may be of great worth in his sight, he may have a purpose for them which gives their lives a very special place in his strategy. Value every child of God: they too have their place in the family.

And let me say a word here to anyone who may have had a bad start in life. You may have been illegitimate and unwanted at the time of your birth. But God wanted you. God had a plan for you. God loved you with a fierce and determined love. If others would reject you he would not for you were precious to him. And so he brought you out into the world and through those early months or perhaps years. They may have been hard years for you, even wretched and sordid ones. But God reached out and took hold of you, washed you clean and made you his, gave you encouragement and told you of his plan for you which led to glory. You are not rejected, you are elect and have been 'from the foundation of the world' (Mt 25:34; Eph 1:4; 1 Pet 1:20).

Letting go the past

I am glad God called Jephthah, and I am glad God called me. You be glad that God has called you. You have a future not just a past; the past is receding every year, the future is drawing nearer; be shaped more and more by your future, leave the things that are behind, let the dead bury their dead, follow Christ:

> There's no discouragement
> Shall make him once relent
> His first avowed intent
> To be a pilgrim.[1]

God was with Jephthah and he became a formidable soldier-leader, albeit of a band of mercenaries, harrying and no doubt pillaging the surrounding tribes who were Israel's constant enemies. Then Jephthah's finest hour comes (Judg 11:4–11): 'Some time later, when the Ammonites made war on Israel, the elders of Gilead went to get Jephthah from the Land of Tob. "Come," they said, "be our commander, so we can fight the Ammonites"' (Judg 4:4–6).

Jephthah faces them with their rejection of him in the past, but they renew their call and agree to make him their leader in a solemn covenant before the Lord. After failing to convince their opponents of their right as a tribe to be left untroubled, we read:

Then the Spirit of the Lord came upon Jephthah. He crossed Gilead and Mannasseh, passed through Mizpah of Gilead, and from there he advanced against the Ammonites. And Jephthah made a vow to the Lord: 'If you give the Ammonites into my hands, whatever comes out of the door of my house to meet me when I return in triumph from the Ammonites will be the Lord's, and I will sacrifice it as a burnt offering.' Then the Lord went over to fight against the Ammonites, and the Lord gave them into his hands ... Thus Israel subdued Ammon. (Judg 11:29–33.)

A fatal and foolish vow

It is at this point that Israel's past catches up with her and generations of decline into superstition and God-forgetfulness exact their price. The defeat of the Ammonites and the joy of Israel should be the climax of the story for the reader but already it is displaced by the reader's anxiety about the vow which Jephthah had made in his hasty and uneducated zeal. The vow is quite unnecessary; God certainly did not require it of him. The form of it is utterly obnoxious to a God holy and good who had forbidden human sacrifice in the Law of Moses and the fulfilment of it is a greater sin, an abomination and a shameful tragedy.

Here we see that Jephthah, splendid as a commander and fine as a politician, is flawed as a spiritual leader and as a private man. His sin however is the sin of Israel as a whole, a sin of the times and the earlier times that bred them. Jephthah is blameworthy but he is also a victim – as much a victim in his way as his daughter who alone comes out faultless.

She comes out on his return home to meet her victorious and honoured father with dancing and tambourines and as he sees his only child and remembers his vows he tears his clothes and cries out: 'Oh! My daughter! You have made me miserable and wretched, because I have made a vow to the Lord that I cannot break' (Judg 11:35).

Her reply ranks her as one of the heroines of Israel and one of the heroes of faith. In innocence more than ignorance she accepts as inevitable the necessity of Jephthah keeping his vow to God and simply says: 'My father, you have given your word to the Lord. Do to me just as you promised, now that the Lord has avenged you of your enemies, the Ammonites. But grant me this request. Give me two months to roam the hills and weep with my friends, because I will never marry' (Judg 7:36–7).

Her untimely death would mean the end of Jephthah's line as well as the denial to her of the happiness of husband and children. Both she and her father are victims:

the hour of bright victory has turned into the darkest hour of their lives.

The silence of God

Where was God in all this? Strangely silent from the start. He knows he is being used, as much as Jephthah was used, by the elders of Gilead (Judg 11:7–11). Consequently, he works only behind the scenes. He sends no prophet (as he did with Deborah and Barak), he makes no personal appearance (as he did with Gideon when the angel of the Lord met him), he gives victory but he does not prevent tragedy. As someone has put it, God's silence is the other side of his anger. God had given Israel his laws, but they had lain neglected and forgotten; he had given them Moses, the greatest of the prophets of whom we read 'The Lord would speak to Moses face to face as a man speaks with his friend' (Ex 33:11), but dark clouds of ignorance and mere folk-religion had rolled over Israel's sky blotting out the face of God.

It is the same with us in our land. How many Bibles do we need only to neglect them; how many prophets only to ignore or resent them? A people who forget God have only themselves to blame when corrupt and cruel elements enter into their religion or their humanism. Jephthah and his daughter fell victim to that.

Did he slay her?

Here however I should mention that there has long been a school of thought which argues that Jephthah did not in fact sacrifice his daughter but consecrated her to perpetual virginity and tabernacle service at Shiloh. Scholars such as Keil and Delitzsch in the last century[2] and Dr Leon Wood in this century[3] have argued their case well. They remind us that such a women's ministry existed (Ex 38:8; 1 Sam 2:22), that human sacrifice was unknown in Israel and would certainly have been condemned with horror by the writer and even the nation (cf. 2 Kings 16:3; 21:6), and that Jephthah's vow in verse 31, if read in the light of the ruling on vows in Leviticus chapter 27, indicates a monetary or other equivalent for what is offered as a sacrifice of thanksgiving to God (e.g. Lev 27:2–4, 14–15). The separate reference in Leviticus 27:29 is to those enemies of God and his people deserving death not to the previous categories of offerings. To us of course Jephthah's daughter will still be seen as the victim of a situation not of her own choosing and one whose loss is very great (Lev 27:37).

However, if Jephthah were here among us now listening to this sermon, I wonder how he would react to these speculations and judgements? If he did sacrifice the life of his own beloved daughter, with her full consent and determination, he might well agree with earnestness that it was wrong; terribly, tragically wrong. Yet I think he might well have stood up by now and said with flashing eye and equal earnestness: 'Is that *all* you have to say about us, that we went wrong, that our times went dark, our faith confused? Don't you recognise, at least, the sincerity, the quality, the *reality* of our faith in the true God. How many of *you* even now, in the full gospel light of Christ which you enjoy, how many of you would sacrifice anything like as much for God? Would some of you sacrifice a single step in your career for God, a wrong relationship for your Lord, even a reputation among your friends as "cool" for the sake of Christ? When is your faith better than mine or stronger or more sacrificial. Don't condemn me – do better than I have done, I and my daughter who loved God too much to let me break my vow.'

Keeping our vows

Let us perhaps examine ourselves in this easy age where vows are unknown beyond the marriage service and often not kept even there. Let us consider the promises we make to God in the hymns and songs we sing and in the prayers and testimonies we make. God is not to be played

159

with: his majesty is colossal, his indignation terrible and his disciplines painful. Better not to make a promise than to break one. Jephthah may teach us the seriousness of faith and his example, tragic as it is, may teach us to think hard before we promise God or make a profession of faith:

> When you make a vow to God, do not delay in fulfilling it. He has no pleasure in fools; fulfil your vow. It is better not to vow than to make a vow and not fulfil it. Do not let your mouth lead you into sin. And do not protest to the temple messenger [or your pastor!] 'My vow was a mistake.' Why should God be angry at what you say and destroy the work of your hands? Much dreaming and many words are meaningless. Therefore stand in awe of God. (Ecc 5:4–7.)

Jesus said we were to count the cost of discipleship (Lk 9:23–6; 14:25–30). In his day and in many parts of the world in our day that cost can be high. A profession of faith in Jesus in some countries can cost you your family, your friends, your university place, your exams, your career, your job, your comfort and even your life. Many know the cost and are prepared to pay it. But many in more liberal societies like our own do not count the cost. Religion for them is 'virtual reality'; an enhanced self image, increased expectations, good songs and nice company.

But when the music stops and the friends are gone and they do not get the job, the girl, the recognition, what then? And when Christ calls them to sacrifice or suffering for him: have they the resources, the bank balance of faith, of prayer, of knowledge of the Scriptures, to win through, to follow on, to overcome the world? I want to say to Jephthah, 'Jephthah, we apologise for our easy superiority, our criticism and our failure to see the root of your faith going deep into God. You deserve your place in Hebrews 11; you and your beautiful daughter.'

160

19

FAITH LEARNING THE HARD WAY (SAMSON)

I am surprised to see Samson's name in Hebrews chapter 11. I would not have put him there, in God's honours list. But then, I am surprised to find my own name in the Lamb's book of life: but there it is in the handwriting of God who loves me, ill-deserving as I am, and I see it clearly whenever I look lovingly, leaningly on Christ his Son, the mirror of my election – and yours.

The story of Samson is the story of squandered gifts and unrealised possibilities. It is also in its own way the story of Israel in the period of the Judges and it can even become your story and mine if we do not walk carefully and in the fear of the Lord. In some ways Samson *is* Israel; the epitome of the nation which gets the judge it deserves, more or less. They could all have been so much more: Samson, Israel, and the men of Dan and Judah. God gave them a door of opportunity but they failed to go through it into conquest and honour and freedom. And so Israel continued to be in thrall to Philistia and God was dishonoured and Dagon elevated.

God is sovereign and unlimited in power but often, because he is the good shepherd of his people, he keeps pace with his sheep and is sadly slowed down by us. How bright in the New Testament history is the presence and power of the kingdom of God, but how wretched has been the history of the institutional Church at times. How easy it is to look back and see superstition and corruption, prejudice and pride, the abandonment of faith's simplicities for fashionable trends of intellectual thought; to see the Church of God 'eyeless in Gaza'. The history of the book of Judges hurts me; the history of the Church hurts me; my own history hurts me; but Hebrews chapter 11 reminds me that 'God has planned something better for us' and that if we 'fix our eyes upon Jesus, the author and perfector of our faith' we too shall stand before him 'at the right hand of the throne of God' (Heb 11:40–12:2)

Early privileges

In Judges chapters 13–16 we are confronted with Samson in all his complexity and contradictions: a man of faith *and* foolishness living a life of faith and failure; a judge in Israel who over his twenty years must have done many good things which are nonetheless overshadowed by some seriously bad ones. And here we find lessons for us all as a result.

The beginning of Samson's story is dominated by God. 'The angel of the Lord' appears to the wife of Manoah announcing that her childlessness is about to be ended, that she is to have a son who has a special destiny in God: 'No razor may be used on his head because the boy is to be a Nazirite, set apart to God from birth, and he will begin the deliverance of Israel from the hands of the Philistines' (Judg 13:5). The word 'Nazirite' means 'consecrated one'. Nazirite vows were usually taken voluntarily and in them a person dedicated themselves to a particular period of prayer and service to God, perhaps for months, perhaps for a number of years, during which they would express their consecration as the Law directed (see Numbers chapter 6), abstaining from alcohol, not cutting their hair and avoiding any contact or even proximity with a dead body. In Samson, as in Samuel later and John the Baptist in New Testament times, we have an example of a Nazirite 'from the womb'. Besides these, others such as Jeremiah (Jer 1:5) and Paul (Gal 1:15), show a deep sense of their lives as having been planned by God, and the Psalmist tells us all that God has a plan for our lives written 'in his book' from the beginning (Ps 139:16). This should be a great encouragement to every one of us.

Speaking personally, I recognise the value of discovering early in life that one has a destiny in God. I think I have wanted to serve God in some capacity since quite a small child. It is a great privilege to know almost from the start what you are put on this earth to do. However, Samson stands as a warning to people like us – that early privileges must not be taken for granted, that gifts and trust and opportunities must be safeguarded not squandered. None of us are safe away from the side of God: the most long-standing Christian leader, the most knowledgeable theologian, the most talented and useful preacher or evangelist, even the most stable of God's servants can fall, can fail, can end their days in tears. Hence Paul writes, urging the Corinthian believers to serious discipleship: 'I beat my body and make it my slave so that after I have preached to others, I myself will not be disqualified for the prize' (1 Cor 9:27). I only wish that Samson had beaten his body; instead he unleashed its drives – and it beat him!

Early follies

Here is another example of a truth we saw earlier in the book: that whenever God tells us to do a thing, Satan is right there to tell us how and when to do it! God had told Samson's parents (who surely told him) that he would begin the deliverance of Israel. In chapter 14 of Judges we find Samson, early in his career, attempting to begin that work. There was a certain amount of uneasy interaction between the Israelites of the tribe of Dan, which was adjacent to Philistia, and the Philistines. As chapter 14 begins we find Samson down in Philistine Timnah (perhaps reconnoitering with a view to his first attack). There he sees a young Philistine girl whom he wants to marry and he asks his parents to begin the customary approach to her family (Judg 14:2).

Samson's parents are dismayed and plead with him: 'Isn't there an acceptable woman among your relatives or among all our people? Must you go to the uncircumcised

Philistines to get a wife?' (Judg 14:3). It is a feature of both Old Testament and New Testament religion that a line is drawn between the people of God and others where marriage is concerned. In the Old Testament God built a wall around Israel – by means of her laws, worship and customs, etc. – which prevented the faith of Israel being influenced, changed and eventually destroyed by the heathen tribes and nations round about her. In Israel alone was the true God known and the salvation of the world, at the coming of the Messiah, depended on that faith being preserved among the chosen people. Similarly in the New Testament period the Apostle Paul writes to the Corinthians: 'Do not be yoked together with unbelievers ... What fellowship can light have with darkness ...? What does a believer have in common with unbelievers?' (2 Cor 6:15).

Pastors know too well the difficulties and dilemmas of mixed marriages where one partner has a supreme loyalty which the other finds threatening or where one partner is notably involved in a church fellowship to which the other is a stranger. Conflict, bafflement and even suspicion can and do breed freely in such a situation. The greatest heartache for the Christian partner however is that the husband or wife they love cannot enter, or even recognise, their greatest joy, their strongest resource and their eternal hope. And then there is the question of the children . . .!

Samson's decision to marry a Philistine will have many repercussions as we can see from chapters 14 and 15. Yet, significantly, Jahweh remains in sovereign control of his life and its effects. Here in our narrative we read that while Samson's motives were mixed and his decision unworthy, yet 'this was from the Lord, who was seeking an occasion to confront the Philistines' (Judg 14:4). God prosecutes his work and forwards his plans even in and through our rebellious ways. That is the guarantee that good shall triumph over evil in the end. It is characteristic of the Old Testament understanding of God that he remains sovereign in every situation, he is not diminished and his purposes are not finally frustrated by human sin.

He himself is uncompromised in his holiness, purity, justice and utter goodness yet he over-rules and somehow uses the follies and failures and even wickedness of men (e.g. Gen 45:4–8). Even the Son of God was betrayed 'by God's set purpose and foreknowledge' (Acts 2:23), those who conspired against him did what God's 'power and will had decided beforehand should happen' (Acts 4:29).

Yet it is a harsh law of life that one bad decision can lead to a whole chain of events which bring their own trouble. The story of Samson's Philistine marriage, the humiliation of the wedding-feast, Samson's revenge, its terrible repercussions for his wife and father-in-law and the great slaughter that followed fill up much of the Samson narrative of chapters 14 and 15. Throughout it all, Samson is seen acting alone. He does not rally his people, dispirited and fearful as they are (15:11); he fights alone, though courageously and in the faith that trusts his God (e.g. Judg 15:11–16). Despite his inconsistencies God is there for him in his times of need (e.g. 15:17–19).

Mid-life crisis – and collapse

Nearly twenty years pass, with Samson as Israel's judge, doing things his way. Yet those years will end with a great reversal, with Samson not dominating but dominated, the prisoner first of his lusts and then of his enemies. The story of his final year or so dominates chapter 16. It begins telling of Samson's night with a Philistine prostitute in a manner which suggests that Samson had never been in control of his sexual passions (Judg 16:1f). It is a shocking thing to come across such a statement in connection with a spiritual leader and, moreover, one whose faith is recorded in Hebrews 11. It was necessary however for it to be clearly recorded as a warning to others, for Samson's sex life was to prove his downfall. Then enters Delilah on the scene (the name approximates to our word 'darling'). His passions are stirred and he falls in love with her. She will be Samson's last passion, his nemesis, his sin and his judgement in one.

We sometimes think we can control sins that are allowed to stay in our lives, but we are mistaken and may be sorely disappointed. There are no 'tame' sins in life. Sin has a life and energy of its own. I remember seeing on the television a clip which showed the importance of vigilance and maximum safety measures for tourists visiting safari parks. A car had been left parked with the window on the driver's seat slightly open. The driver's seat was occupied by a dummy. A nearby camera filmed the outcome. At first the approaching lioness, looking so sleek and calm and rather beautiful, just walked around the vehicle sniffing curiously until she realised that the window was open and the figure within was in reach. Quick as a flash and without warning her strong paw was in at the window and the figure was pulled out to be immediately torn apart by the lioness. A slow, unthreatening creature had became a snarling fury in seconds.

Sin can be like that: lust, pride, greed and jealousy can spring out of control after years of controlled indulgence, taking us over the edge into disaster. Samson found this after his pillow-talk with his mistress led to him betraying to her the secret of his strength: 'So he told her everything, "No razor has ever been used on my head" he said "because I have been a Nazirite, set apart to God since birth. If my head were shaved my strength would leave me and I would become as weak as any other man"' (Judg 16:17). Delilah herself was controlled by others, their bribe was huge, her opportunity to rid her people of their great scourge was unique and her decision was fatal to Samson whose extraordinary and charismatic ministry was doomed.

Samson's strength was not his own. It was 'hung in his hair' – not literally or biologically of course but symbolically. His Nazirite hair had a sacramental character, it was the outward sign of an invisible gift. His great strength was supernatural and depended on his relationship to God. That relationship had held, with little thanks to Samson, for nearly twenty years though under many strains. But when Samson sold out to Delilah the Philis-

166

tine and the vow was finally broken, then the Spirit of God departed and so also did Samson's strength.

Playing fast and loose – bound hand and foot

In this Samson was again a sign to Israel – and to us. Without God he was 'as other men'. And without Jahweh Israel was 'as other nations'. Only Jahweh was their unique excellence; their God was their glory. So it is with you and me as believers. Around us are many men and women who are stronger than we are, cleverer than we are, even better people than we are. But while we have *God*, we have the better portion. However, if we lose him we lose our great distinction and privilege; we become 'as other men' and in fact we become less. Surely chapter 16:20 is a text we should remember with fear: 'He awoke from his sleep and thought, "I'll go out as before and shake myself free." But he did not know that the Lord had left him.'

We may not at first see how compromise weakens us; nor may we see it even when we have passed the fatal point. But there comes a time, a terrible time of realisation, when we find we cannot do what we once could do, and worse, can no longer be what we once were. We cannot step backwards into our old self or situation. We have become strangers to ourselves. There are serious lessons for us all here and especially for leaders in churches. If we play fast and loose with the gifts of God we may lose both the gifts and God! We cannot love both God and the world which hates his ways (1 Jn 2:15–17), we cannot live in blessing and backsliding together, and those of us who lead in spiritual things must always remember that we lose our ministry if we lose our integrity.

So at the story's end we find Samson 'Eyeless in Gaza, at the mill with slaves'.[1] I recall reading of a sermon once preached from the life of Samson on the danger of sin. It had three unforgettable headings: *sin blinds*, *sin binds*, *sin grinds*. As we see this once great man lumbering around in servitude, blinded and helpless, we are surely led to cry out to God that he who saved us would keep us from sin's power and temptation's danger.

His last act

Yet, God had not finished with Samson or with Israel. He who was at the beginning of the story was at the end too, for Samson's hair began to grow again and the Spirit of God returning met Samson's last prayer with mighty power (Judg 16:28). It was at a great feast given by the Philistines in praise of Dagon their god for delivering Samson into their hands. Thousands crowded the temple roof and precincts and as a climax to the festivities Samson, blind and helpless, was led out by 'the servant who held his hand' to entertain the mocking crowds he could not see.

During a respite under the portico of the proper temple, Samson asks the servant to put his hand to the main pillars of the great house. As he prays for the return of the miraculous strength that had once marked his ministry in Israel, the Spirit of God descends upon him in one last act of power. Samson, tragic and heroic, prays again, '"Let me die with the Philistines!" Then he pushed with all his might and down came the temple on the rulers and all the people in it. Thus he killed many more when he died than while he lived' (Judg 16:30).

So the God of Israel confirmed the age-old promise given to Abraham and Moses and Joshua: that their enemies would be his enemies and the land and the future would be theirs. Even the failures of the past would not annul the blessing of the future, 'for God's gifts and his call are irrevocable' (Rom 11:29).

Faith's might-have-been

From Samson we learn what faith might have been but never was. His final conquest does not make up for his many failures. That faith could live and make a final conquest in his life is a lesson in the matchless patience and unfailing love of God: 'If we are faithless, he will remain faithful for he cannot deny himself' (2 Tim 2:13).

God can sustain faith even when it is neglected and can painfully, patiently await his hour. Here then we have a strange, a sobering but also an encouraging lesson in faith. Faith has this quality and this distinguishing feature: that though it is starved and beaten and mistreated, though it is put away in a drawer, packed up in the attic and dragged through situations which are utterly inimical to it, yet in the goodness and mercy of God it can survive and surface and finally assert itself.

We have all known Christians who made a bad decision – or a series of bad decisions – not innocently but wilfully, rebelliously, determinedly. Perhaps it was a connection with career advancement or it may have been in the choice of a spouse or it may have involved a particular legal or ethical matter. At the time it suited them and for a while they prospered, but what years of sorrow and spiritual starvation it led them into! And at the end, maybe at the end of a life, in the everlasting mercy of God someone was sent to minister to them, to rake over the ashes of their soul in hope of finding some remnant of faith, and the Spirit blew and a tiny flame emerged and they died in repentant faith, hobbling home to heaven, saved but only just.

And so Samson hobbled home, a big lumbering giant of a man, God's athlete, crippled by his own foolishness, God's strong man reduced to near helplessness by his own bad decisions. Take care with your present spiritual strength; it is not inexhaustible. It is a growing principle but do not let life stunt it. It is there and it will live – but the great question now is *how* will it live: as a slave to the Philistines or as God's free and faithful servant?

20

FAITH RECOVERING (SAMUEL)

In Hebrews 11:32 Samuel is placed after David because the writer wants to class him among the prophets. In fact Samuel was both a judge and a prophet: the last of the Judges and the first of the major Old Testament prophets that followed over the centuries. It is as a prophet that Samuel is so significant in terms of the history of salvation that we have in the Old Testament.

A nation under judgement

The period of the Judges was, as we have seen, a grim and tragic period in Israel's history. The law of God was largely forgotten, religion had become adulterated with Baal-worship from the surrounding tribes and debased by superstition, and morality was at a wretchedly low standard. As a divine rebuke to such national backsliding God withdrew his Spirit and 'the word of the Lord was rare, there were not many visions' (1 Sam 3:1). The epitaph of the entire period is found in Judges 21:25 – 'In those days Israel had no king; everyone did as he saw fit.' Those last words remind us of the epitaph that our own generation is choosing for itself: 'I did it my way!' Surely an epitaph without regret, without enlightenment and without hope.

The silent God

'The boy Samuel ministered before the Lord under Eli. In those days the word of the Lord was rare; there were not many visions' (1 Sam 3:l). God was not completely silent of course, nor entirely absent from Israel as we have read in the book of Judges. Yet these words were both ominous and tragic: ominous because God's judgement was involved here, tragic because the situation was so unnecessary and so far from Israel's privilege and possibilities.

One of the greatest judgements God can inflict on anyone is to leave them to themselves without restraint, without check or challenge. In the first chapter of his letter to the Romans the Apostle Paul speaks of God's response to those who 'suppress the knowledge of God in their hearts and lives ... Who exchange the truth of God for a lie, and worship and serve created things rather than the Creator' (Rom 1:18, 25). As a mark of his wrath and as part of the process of judgement God 'gave them over to shameful lust' and to 'a depraved mind' to do and to defend and even promote what ought not to be done (Rom 1:26, 28, 32). When light recedes darkness advances and so when God withdraws, angered and grieved, those who have defied him 'become filled with every kind of wickedness': envy, murder, strife, deceit and malice (Rom 1:29). The God-haters become man-haters and in the end, perhaps, selfhaters: 'senseless, faithless, heartless, ruthless' (Rom 1:31).

When a society displaces God, self is not big enough to fill the space and many things rush in to fill the vacuum besides the things we want. Dark forces, competing interests, alien 'values' and perverted norms all claim their place and their opportunity to dominate. Evil cannot be localised, sin cannot be tamed and a society cannot be selectively permissive for long. The judgement of God is not necessarily – or even usually – conveyed in lightening bolts; his wrath 'goes out' (Rom 1:18) every day in silent ways but they are no less terrible for all that.

A church under judgement

As one of the greatest judgements God can inflict on a society is his withdrawal from its central, conscious life, so correspondingly, one of the greatest judgements God can inflict on the Church is his silence. It was a greater evil and disgrace for *Israel* to sink as low as it did than it would have been for any other nation. For Israel had known the true God and his ways; Israel had had such patriarchs as Moses and Joshua. Israel had been the most favoured of nations. Other tribes and peoples had only the legacies of men, the folklore of a fallen people, the false pride or degrading immorality or bloody terror of debased religion. But Israel had the true God and his salvation. Paul could say, centuries later: 'Theirs is the adoption as sons; theirs the divine glory, the covenants, the receiving of the law, the temple worship and the promises. Theirs are the patriarchs and from them is traced the human ancestry of Christ who is God over all, for ever praised' (Rom 9:4–5).

To sin against such light is sin indeed; to turn true religion into false is a terrible alchemy; it is to fall under the curse of Christ's word – 'If the light which is in you is darkness, how great is that darkness.' When God judges the Church, he does not send thunder but silence; the Spirit is grieved; the blessing is withdrawn. The Church experiences loss of vision, loss of power, loss of credibility – her own life has become impoverished; she can never be riches to the world. The prophet Amos warned another backslidden generation:

'The days are coming,' declares the Sovereign Lord, 'when I will send a famine through the land – not a famine of food or a thirst for water, but a famine of hearing the words of the Lord. Men will stagger from sea to sea and wander from north to east searching for the words of the Lord, but they will not find it.' (Amos 8:11–12).

With the loss of God's word we experience the loss of certainty, the frustration of needing to know the truth and always seeking it yet never finding it – because the truth we need is the truth we have rejected and our quest for an alternative truth is the quest for non-existent 'holy grail'. With the loss of God's word we are thrown upon each other's word or our own word; and what sort of a bargain is that? And so our modern world has 'exchanged the truth of God for the lie' of a Godless secularism, of an atheistic humanism, of materialism and now of mysticism. Ideologies, scientisms and, more recently, 'new-age' superstitions have all been tried but all are doomed to disappoint.

It is in the nature of God however, and a feature of his work in history, that when a society is crumbling on its inadequate foundations God is always ready to do a new work there, ready to step into the rubble and rebuild. Then he becomes, once again, the speaking God.

The speaking God

> One night Eli, whose eyes were becoming so weak that he could barely see, was lying down in his usual place. The lamp of God had not yet gone out and Samuel was lying down in the temple of the Lord, where the ark was. Then the Lord called Samuel. (1 Sam 3:2–4.)

Notice that it is God who makes the first move. He it is who breaks the long silence of his indignation. He is not petitioned by a national repentance; the priests are not transformed nor is there a reformation which first of all sweeps out Eli's sons and their corruption. But God in sovereign grace chooses to act, to break the deadlock and to advance the plan of salvation-history for the redemption of the world. And the point of his entry will be the sleepy half-consciousness of a youth, Samuel the boy of the temple. It will be so sudden and so new to him this voice of prophecy, that Samuel will at first mistake it for the voice of the old priest Eli. But it is the voice of God and the announcement of a new era. Eli represents the past, Samuel represents the future. The past is never as good as we like to remember and here for two hundred years and more it has been a sorry tale. Eli is the end of an era; Samuel is the beginning. Samuel in his sweet and vulnerable childhood is the first flower of spring, a protected young plant which will grow into a strong tree.

Here we have the story of every revival in the history of the Church. They are usually preceded by a period of decline, of apathy and spiritual ignorance. Then God chooses a Martin Luther or a George Whitefield or a Hugh Bourne or an Evan Roberts. Revivals have often begun with unknown men and women and small groups of praying people. They seemed unlikely instruments of power. But once again 'God chose the foolish things of the world to shame the wise; God chose the weak things of the world to shame the strong' (1 Cor 1:27).

We have to admit, sorrowfully, that in the Church as well as in the world there is a tendency to 'run down', to decline, to weaken because of sin. The law of sin brought with it a kind of spiritual entropy of which we are not yet quite free. We too can be wound up on Sunday and run down by Friday. We can have our evangelical high days in festivals at Minehead or Keswick or we can feel 'topped up' from a mission or a period of service. And afterwards, as the world exhausts us or tempts us, we can find faith running low and devotion cooling and an attraction to lesser or unprofitable things growing.

In God however there is a determination to keep a Church, a true Church in the world until the final day of salvation and judgement (Mt 16:18). That Church has often become worldly, corrupt, apathetic, superstitious, nominal. And God has brought judgement upon it. Yet God has not let judgement be the last word. He has revived his Church and sent times of reformation, refreshing and revival; new life, new leadership, new vision. The Church too has had a 'Judges' period of decline and disgrace but God, in wonderful grace and forgiveness, has led that Church out of the wilderness into his green pastures. Jesus Christ is the guide and guarantee of that salvation-history which is God's path through the centuries.

And all this is true of the individual believer. In ourselves there are possibilities of great goodness and great badness, of faithfulness and of backsliding. Like Israel we can be a light to the nations or a disgrace to our calling. We need the grace of God every day of our lives, the grip of Christ on us and the Holy Spirit filling us (Eph 1:17; 5:18). Sometimes we forget the lessons and experiences of our past and fall into periods of spiritual decline and personal failure. Then God does a new thing in our lives: his speech breaks the silence and his words are, astonishingly, not words of final condemnation but of love and a renewed invitation to walk again in his company and in a new direction. God is the God of new beginnings for us all, the God who recovers us, the God who can change us. 'His anger lasts only a moment but his favour lasts for a lifetime' (Ps 30:5). He 'longs to be gracious' (Is 30:18). He meets us in our sin and need and failure not to mock us but to mend us, to lift us, to set us on our feet and take us on from failure to success.

A listening people

When God comes to Samuel it is not in the splendour of the throne-room of heaven and it is not in a voice of thunder. The door posts of the Tabernacle do not shake and there is no rushing mighty wind to extinguish the temple lamp. There is only a quiet persistent voice in the softened darkness calling a name, 'Samuel, Samuel.' There are many calls of God in the Old Testament, all of them different. He called Moses from a desert bush burning with strange fire (Ex 3). He called Isaiah from the holy majesty of his throne room (Is 6). He called Ezekiel from the centre of an inexpressible glory (Ezek 1). He called Samuel in a way so ordinary, so lacking in splendour or terror, that the youth thought it was the old man in the next room!

Be alert to the calls of God in your life. Do not demand drama or a repetition of another's experience. Let God come to you as he wills and let him find you listening. He may meet you and call you to a particular work in the sermon or the songs of a church service, or as you read the Bible or pray alone, by a sudden realisation or growing awareness, from the pages of a book or a conversation in

176

the street. God called Samuel in a voice so human he could not tell it from Eli's; and God may speak to you in the accent and words of your best friend or a relative or a pastor.

It is not up to us how God speaks to us; our business is to cultivate a listening spirit, a waiting, open heart. He is the person-to-person God who works differently in every life and meets us in numberless ways. You and I often complain of his silence when the problem is our deafness! Let God speak to you in familiar ways and you will find him vocal enough and his words weighty with encouragement and challenge. What he requires of you first and foremost is the attitude which says: 'Speak, Lord, for your servant is listening.'

21

FAITH GAINING CONTROL
(DAVID)

'And what more shall I say? I do not have time to tell about Gideon, Barak, Samson, Jephthah, David, Samuel and the prophets . . .'(Heb 11:32).

After the period of the Judges, a wretched couple of centuries in Israel's history, the people demanded a king. It had been God's intention to give them, in time, a king and a unique kind of monarchy – one which would be subject to him and one which would reflect his own kingship (Deut 17:14–20). But the people, without consideration of this, approached Samuel the prophet, now an old man, and demanded, 'Now appoint us a king to lead us, such as all the nations have' (1 Sam 8:5). In this they were wrong, both in their model and their motive. Their model was not God but the tribal strength and structures of the nations around them and their motive was to be like them.

In the event God, after due warning, gave them a king 'such as all the other nations' had, and Saul son of Kish the Benjamite became their king. God gave Saul every means to rule well: the support of Samuel, the anointing of the Holy Spirit, the backing of the tribes and his first victory over Israel's enemies.

A secular man in a sacred society

However from the beginning Saul was a flawed man. He was a secular man in a sacred society. He himself does not appear to have been a deeply religious man (1 Sam 9:5–6) and it is precisely here that he fell down. As a leader he had great qualities, as a commander of armies he was a charismatic personality and fine strategist. But every time he tried to be religious he fell flat on his face!

179

His basic trouble was that he thought he could control situations spiritually as he controlled situations politically and militarily. He attempted early on to substitute for the absent Samuel by performing priestly functions and sacrifice before a major battle when he had been told to wait (1 Sam 13:1–14) and at another time he set aside the directive of God in his conquest of the Amalekites (1 Sam 15:1–29). The significance of these acts was greater than might at first appear. They show at a very early stage the tension between king and cultus, between palace and temple, that would surface again and again in the centuries that followed. Saul tried to extend the power of the kingship into the religious life of Israel, into areas where it had no mandate. The separation of the functions of king and priest was, in part, God's way of limiting the monarchy and of keeping it in proper subjection to his law. Other kings too would find that restraint irksome.

It is at this point that our study of David begins. After Saul's failure and disobedience God makes it clear to Samuel that he has a new beginning in store for Israel and the monarchy: 'The Lord said to Samuel, "How long will you mourn for Saul, since I have rejected him as king over Israel? Fill your horn with oil and be on your way; I am sending you to Jesse of Bethlehem, I have chosen one of his sons to be king"' (1 Sam 16:1). The story that follows is well known: of Samuel being attracted by the visible strength and qualities of Jesse's seven sons and learning that 'The Lord does not look at the things man looks at. Man looks at the outward appearance, but the Lord looks at the heart' (1 Sam 16:7). Eventually David, the youngest, is brought in from his sheep-tending, Samuel is told, 'Rise and anoint him; he is the one' (1 Sam 16:12) and 'from that day on the Spirit of the Lord came on David in power' (1 Sam 16:13).

A king without a crown

From this point David is king-in-waiting, a king without a crown – anonymous but elect. As for Saul, he gradually declines into madness and paranoia. The story continues with David coming to the court (1 Sam 16–17) and Saul's growing jealousy and his attempts to kill David who becomes the great warrior, the scourge of the Philistines and the darling of the crowds who cry, 'Saul has slain his thousands, David his tens of thousands.'

Eventually David is forced to flee for his life. No longer the unnoticed shepherd boy on the Bethlehem hills, he is now the best-known man in Israel, a national hero (remember Goliath?) and a seasoned warrior. Yet in a sickening reversal of fortunes he becomes again David the nobody, the outlaw, the fugitive. For years he is exiled from home and kept from the destiny God promised him: hounded by Saul and his troops he makes some bad and foolish decisions (including living for a while with his old enemy the Philistines [1 Sam 21; 27]). Many of his psalms were written in this bleak period of his life, psalms of trial and of trust, psalms of tears and disappointment, yet also psalms of survival (e.g. Psalms 18; 34; 52; 56; 57; 59). Israel now has two kings: one installed and one anointed; one in the place of power and one in the purposes of God; Saul, who has kept the crown but lost the glory and David, who is exiled from court but has the unfailing presence of God who has gone into exile with him. It is sad to read of Saul spiralling down into madness and apostasy; and the years of David's flight and struggles for survival were wretched rather than romantic.

Empowered for service

We tend to think that 'an anointing with power' (1 Sam 16:13) is the end of struggle and setback. However the readers of Hebrews were being taught a lesson we too must learn – that we are anointed for conflict not for comfort, prepared for spiritual warfare not tranquility, empowered for service not for status (Heb 10:32–9). A notable New Testament commentary on that is the life of the Apostle Paul from its beginning (Acts 9:16), through long years of apostolic ministry (2 Cor 5:3–10; 11:23–8).

181

Paul saw his sufferings as being the ongoing sufferings of Christ in his people (2 Cor 1:5), and David himself, in his own experience, suffered 'such opposition from sinful men' as our Lord endured, and often faced weariness and discouragement (Heb 12:3).

Yet it is better to be David in the wilderness than Saul in the palace; better to have nothing but God than to have everything except God. A man or woman who like Saul has everything in life except God, has very little for long: beauty fades, brain falters, careers end and death makes the final judgement on their priorities. A man or woman who like David has God, may lose a great deal: career prospects may never materialise, daily life may be a struggle and frustration, sickness, age and finally death may come. But they have God who has said, 'Never will I leave you; never will I forsake you' (Heb 13:5). They will serve *his* purposes and death itself will not be a defeat but an entrance into glory and eternal gain.

Our goals must never be our gods

During the years of David's exile and flight from Saul there were two occasions when David and his men might easily have assassinated the half-mad rejected king (1 Sam 24 and 26). Yet David was continually aware that Saul had once been anointed king at the command of God and that the Spirit of God had sealed or confirmed it. Consequently David always recognised Saul's kingship as legitimate, and even sacred, as long as he lived. David was never a threat to Saul but Saul, ever more unstable, could never see that. When David's own men encouraged him to kill Saul when he had opportunity he replied: 'The Lord forbid that I should do such a thing to my master, the Lord's anointed, or lift my hand against him; for he is the anointed of the Lord' (1 Sam 24:7).

David was destined for the throne of Israel. That destiny was delayed and blocked by Saul. Yet David would not take the throne wrongly, he would not wade to it through blood, he would not achieve his goals at all costs.

This teaches us that God's will must be done in God's way or it will not really be done at all. We cannot help the cause of God by doing evil that good may come of it; we cannot compensate for sin *now* by righteousness *then*. We must at each stage do the right thing and leave the issue of it to God. We all have goals but our goals must never be our gods. David's God was more important than his goals and God must be more important to us than our goals. Even when faith, and not mere ambition, has seen and set before itself the undoubted goals of God, its work has only begun.

In going for God's goals there are often irksome delays and sometimes fatal short-cuts! To get to the goal in the wrong way can be to damage or even destroy the goal before you get there. Perhaps it will be you who will be damaged or even destroyed. It may be a different 'you' who reaches the goal you pursued so ruthlessly and a 'you' unable to do much to the glory of God or for the help of his kingdom after all. This has been the story of thousands. David, with Saul's blood on his hands, would not have been 'the man after God's own heart' (1 Sam 13:14).

David's greatest conquest – and ours

David made many conquests when he came to the throne but he made his greatest conquest before that time. His character was tempered and formed in the hard and lonely years being hunted by Saul 'as one hunts a partridge in the mountains' (1 Sam 26:20). There he learned to curb his passion and deal with his bitterness. It was easier for David to conquer Goliath than to conquer David. David had to learn to rule himself before he was ready to rule a kingdom: 'Better is a patient man than a warrior, a man who controls his temper than one who takes a city' (Prov 16:32).

It is one of the great characteristics of God's people that the grace of God works in them as a power 'to will and to do his good pleasure' (Phil 2:12 13; cf. Gal 2:20). It is a power above fallen human nature. In the case of David and Saul, human nature said, 'Strike him'; the power of grace said, 'Spare him'; human nature said, 'Despise him for what he is'; the power of grace said, 'Honour him for what he represents'; human nature said, 'He is your enemy'; the power of grace said, 'He is the Lord's anointed.'

The significance of Saul's office as king went far beyond his personal worthiness or descent (cf. Rom 13:1). David refused to take revenge. Revenge is a poisonous thing. It is sweet to the mouth but bitter to the stomach. Patience, meekness, forgiveness are often hard to exercise at the time of injury but when remembered later they bring satisfaction and peace and leave no regret. Did you ever regret them? But have you not often regretted displaying their opposites?

In the obedience of faith, David eventually got his throne (Saul was slain by his own hand after battle with the Philistines, 1 Sam 31:1–6) and became Israel's greatest king. His name and history are invoked here in Hebrews chapter 11 because these Jewish believers are, like David, anointed by God but hated and persecuted by an irrational and obsessive unbelief in their fellow countrymen. The glory of God is promised them for the future, but exile and disgrace suffered for the name of Christ is the present reality. They are urged to look with the eyes of faith, to live as 'seeing' what God has promised, and to bear with dignity the time of their exile: 'Let us, then, go to him outside the camp, bearing the disgrace he bore. For here we have no enduring city, but we are looking for the city that is to come' (Heb 13:13–14).

22

FAITH LOSING CONTROL
(DAVID)

King David is in his early forties. At last all the tribes are
content with his rule and he is at peace in his capital city,
Jerusalem. However, it seems that for kings to keep the
peace they must go to war and at the time our story opens
David has sent his armies out on their spring offensive
against Israel's traditional enemies – the Ammonites.
David, however, is learning to be a real king and conducts
this war by proxy, remaining in Jerusalem in comfort and
state! (2 Samuel 11.)

This is why he is the wrong man in the wrong place
when, unable to sleep and walking on the flat roof of the
royal residence he sees the beautiful wife of one of his
captains, ritually bathing after her monthly period. Having
seen what was happening he should have turned away
immediately, leaving her in her privacy and dignity, but
the glance became a gaze and the walls of resolution and
self-control began to crack.

When a glance becomes a gaze

I think it was Billy Graham who once said, 'You can't
help the first look; you can help the second', and each
glance thereafter leaves you weaker and the temptation
stronger. Nowadays we can have David's experience at
the touch of a button as television produces its soft porn
for general entertainment. So sex is degraded, privacy is
exploited, the Spirit is grieved, the mind is stained and the
passions are aroused. It may not be real but it is not
thereby harmless; for fantasy is a kind of reality and
thoughts are things.

Fantasy is not just a toy; it can be a fire – and who can say where it will end? Jesus warned us of an adultery of the heart (Mt 5:28), a kind of mental rape in which God is insulted and an innocent person degraded. His reference, it is true, is more directly to lusting for a known person than a screen image or a fictional character, yet there too the mind is stained and the Spirit grieved and who can say what will follow a surrender to the latter when the temptation to the former presents itself?

Moreover we will learn from what follows that you cannot simply 'confine' sin to one thing. Its effect on a person's character and on their spiritual and moral health affects other things in turn. In David's case we shall find self-indulgence falling prey to lust, lust leading to adultery and adultery covered up first with lies and finally with murder. This is the kind of progression that sin with its primitive energies and appetites is capable of making, taking events out of our control. We can see this happening in the disastrous 'permissive society', which is still with us, in its marriage break-up, its increasing violence and manslaughter. A society cannot choose to be permissive in one thing; sin is a growing force which soon bursts its bounds and runs in other directions than the one chosen for it.

The second step to ruin

Verse three shows us David's second step to ruin. He should not have played the voyeur but now he goes one decisive step nearer – he sends someone 'to find out about her' (2 Sam 11:3). Now David already has wives and also a harem of concubines according to the lamentable standards of the time. His wives include the beautiful and intelligent Abigail; but 'stolen waters are sweet and bread eaten in secret is delightful' (Prov 9:17). David was a lost man the moment he sent someone to find out about her and by the time he sent for her to come to him he was out of control.

Lois Mowday in her perceptive and excellent book *The Snare* says that 'Immorality is a process' and explains:

> Even the proverbial 'one night stand' didn't just happen in a chance meeting. A whole series of events caused that evening of sin. Without a doubt, the people involved became aware at *some point along the way* that they are being disobedient and that they are beginning to reach the point of no return.[1]

Lois Mowday brings home her lesson that immorality is a process by adding the warning, '*Any of us could be in the process right now.*'

David has controlled so much but now something is controlling him: 'Like a city whose walls are broken down is a man who lacks self-control' (Prov 25:28). The information that comes back places David's next step beyond the pale. This is no local girl, no 'available' virgin, but another man's wife. And that man is one of his own soldiers.

The seduction is recorded very briefly (with the heavy irony that Bathsheba had 'purified herself from her uncleanness'). David sent for her. She came to him. He slept with her. 'Then she went back home.' David thinks he can resume normal life and for a time he does. Then comes the brief but devastating message: 'I am pregnant,' and in those three words (two in the Hebrew) David's confidence is shaken and his world threatened. This is but an extreme and well-known instance of sin's knock-on effect, its continuing power in consequences that lie beyond anyone's control. The consequences of this sin will live as long as David lives – and, alas, for longer than Uriah will live.

The cover up

Chapter 11 of 2 Samuel, verses 6–13 record David's first and futile attempt to cover up what he has done. He summons Uriah from the front and tries to get him to sleep with his wife so that the child will be assumed to be Uriah's. But Uriah is a better man than David thinks and refuses the joys of home while his fellow soldiers are at the front. The story leads on to David's final, desperate solution. It is a terrible and shameful solution; a contradiction of everything he stands for as a man of God, an Israelite king and a great army general. Verses 14–27 tell for all time David's blackest crime – murder by proxy to prevent Uriah finding out, and yet a deed guaranteed to become known as all such crimes tend to become known. David the great commander engineers the death of one of his finest and most loyal captains.

'Am I a dog that I should so such a thing?' David might have said before the chain of events. Yet one sin can make way for another and a greater and we can all find ourselves *where* we never thought we could be and *what* we never thought we could be.

Almost a year follows and by the time Nathan the prophet exposes David the child has been born. But what a year it must have been: a year of repressed guilt, of palace intrigue, of public hypocrisy. I can imagine at any of the great national festivals in Jerusalem people crowding forward to catch a glimpse of Israel's king and sweet psalmist in the processions, lifting their children to see 'the man after God's own heart', looking on in admiration and pride. But it was no longer the old David they were looking at; it was a psalm-less king, a guilty man, an adulterer and murderer. Joab, David's clever and ruthless right-hand man knew it, Bathsheba knew at least part of it and David knew it.

Exposure

At last, after the growing strain of that Godless, cheerless, guilt-ridden year, God sends his prophet Nathan to break the silence, to lance the boil. Nathan tells the story of a rich man who plundered a poor one of his only lamb – 'one little ewe lamb' – which the poor man raised: 'It shared his food, drank from his cup and even slept in his

188

arms' (2 Sam 12:3). David walks right into the trap: 'As surely as the Lord lives, the man who did this deserves to die!' Nathan is ready as God's spokesman to spring the trap: 'Then Nathan said to David, "You are the man"' (2 Sam 12:7).

No doubt it was a risky thing to do: confronting such a grossly backslidden king with such a stark truth, but Nathan did it and did it with a divine authority that utterly overcame David. In that moment David breaks and the king becomes the shepherd boy again; walls of rebellion and towers of pride crumble as Nathan adds charge to charge and announces the consequences in David's life and among his family (2 Sam 12:7–12), and David confesses his sin, 'Then David said to Nathan, "I have sinned against the Lord"' (2 Sam 12:13).

The cost of forgiveness

You and I might have prescribed a long period of penance to follow such a sin, a trial period to test the truth of his sorrow, a period 'on probation' before David was fully released into peace and service. That is not God's way. '"In a surge of anger I hid my face from you for a moment, but with everlasting kindness I will have compassion on you," says the Lord your Redeemer (Is 54:8). As soon as David confesses his sin Nathan pronounces absolution: 'Nathan replied, "The Lord has taken away your sin"' (2 Sam 12:13). In a moment, it seems, David is forgiven! The chains fall off, the ice melts, the spirit returns, the darkness lifts. David will sing his great psalm of repentance (Psalm 51) and write others too (e.g. Psalm 32). David will be great again – but only because 'great David's greater son' will humble himself unto death. It is Jesus who will sweat in Gethsemane and die on Golgotha for David's sin. David's prayer will be answered when he cries, 'Do not cast me from your presence' but only because Another standing in his name and place would one day cry, 'My God, my God, why have you foresaken me?' (Mt 27:45). The ground and basis of David's forgiveness and justification is the same as our own. In the words of the Apostle Paul: 'God made him who had no sin to be sin for us, so that in him we might become the righteousness of God' (2 Cor 5:21).

I often quote some bold words of Martin Luther on the atoning work of Christ which bring together Old and New Testament and show Christ crucified as the basis of both:

> God sent his only Son into the world and laid upon him all the sins of all men, saying 'Be Thou Peter, that denier; Paul, that persecutor, blasphemer and cruel oppressor; David that adulterer; that sinner who did eat of the forbidden fruit in Paradise; that thief who hung upon the cross ... be Thou the Person who has committed the sins of all men; see therefore that you pay and satisfy for them.'

Luther concludes:

> By this means the whole world is purged and cleansed from all sins and so delivered from death and all evils. Now sin being vanquished and death abolished by this one Man, God would see nothing else in the whole world, if it did believe, than mere cleansing and righteousness.[2]

Without this where would any of us be? Surely under a great condemnation and doomed to a terrible eternity 'for all have sinned and fall short of the glory of God' (Rom 3:23). With this, however, we have a gospel for the whole world as those who 'are justified freely by his grace' (Rom 3:24). Consequently we have a testimony to give that 'burdens are lifted at Calvary', that Christ can make 'the foulest clean' that with him on our side we can approach the judgement seat of God with confidence and gratitude:

> The vilest offender who truly believes
> That moment from Jesus a pardon receives.[3]

The consequence of sin

Of David however, one more thing must be said. His sin, even though forgiven, had ongoing and dire consequences, as Nathan had predicted: 'Now therefore the sword shall never depart from your house, because you despised me and took the wife of Uriah the Hittite to be your own ... Out of your own household I am going to bring calamity upon you. Before your very eyes I will take your wives and give them to one who is close to you, and he will lie with your wives in broad daylight ... because by doing this you have made the enemies of the Lord show utter contempt, the son born to you will die' (2 Sam 12:10–14).

So it all came to pass. In the years that followed, Jerusalem would house rival factions among David's children by his different wives and the man who could rule a nation well would show himself unable to govern his own family with firmness. To the end of the record we encounter trouble and tragedy. David's first son Amnon would rape his half-sister Tamar. David's second son Absalom would kill Amnon for the rape – Tamar being Absalom's full sister. Absalom himself would plot and plan and win over the hearts of the people in a successful rebellion and for a short time would even occupy Jerusalem itself, taking David's harem as his own while David fled with his loyal troops. Even after his death at the hands of Joab, the sword did not depart from David's house and things were never quite the same again.

No one can know in advance or measure the consequences of sin. Do you know the longest recorded shadow in the physical world? It is the shadow cast by a mountain in Tenerife, the El Piton Peak. The peak rises sharply twelve thousand two hundred feet above the Atlantic and at sunrise and sunset casts a shadow nearly one hundred and fifty miles long! In the moral world however, sin casts longer shadows by far than that: successions of lovelessness, pride and vice that run through generations from parents to children can cast grim shadows across a hundred years and more. Injustice breeds injustice and an entire nation can spiral down into corruption and on into generations of poverty and despair. Perhaps the reason that the day of judgement is left until the last day is because sin's full effects can only be measured at the end of a fallen world's history.

However, after the death of David and Bathsheba's child, we read:

> Then David comforted his wife Bathsheba, and he went into her and lay with her. She gave birth to a son and they named him Solomon. The Lord loved him; and because the Lord loved him, he sent word through Nathan the prophet to name him Jedidiah ('loved by the Lord'). (2 Sam 12:24–5).

So we discover that God does not let sin have the last word among his people or his purposes. Here is the promise of a new beginning even out of a sorry ending, a promise of victory plucked out of defeat: God's victory out of our defeats.

23

FAITH SUFFERING
(HEB 11:33–8)

We must never forget as we read this great chapter that it is written to a suffering Church. The writer is reminding them of past heroes of faith not as entertainment but as strong encouragement in a desperate hour. He had written earlier:

> Remember those earlier days after you had received the light, when you stood your ground in a great contest in the face of suffering. Sometimes you were publicly exposed to insult and persecution; at other times you stood side by side with those so treated. You sympathised with those in prison and joyfully accepted the confiscation of your property because you knew that you yourself had better and lasting possessions. So do not throw away your confidence; it will be richly rewarded. (Heb 10:32–5.)

These early Christian believers were born again into turmoil. We tend to wrap up and protect our new converts in many ways. They however were warned about trials and persecutions from the start (Mt 10:34–39; cf. Jn 15:18–21; Acts 9:15–16). Someone has said that Jesus promised his people three things: that they would be in constant trouble, completely fearless and absurdly happy. The poetic licence involved does not preclude the other side of suffering: fear, depression and the temptation to abandon faith or at least its open profession.

These Hebrew Christians have been through all the stages including the last, and our writer having warned them against 'drifting away' (Heb 2:1), outright apostacy (Heb 6:4–8), and giving up their meeting together (Heb 10:25), reassures them that 'in just a very little while' Christ will come again to rescue and vindicate his people and warns them that his judgements will be far worse than anything their persecutors can inflict (Heb 10:37–39). Then he launches into his brief history of great men and women of faith who believed the promises of God and endured.

For many of us today in the liberal democracies of the West, the biblical references to persecution for Christ's sake seem somewhat remote and unreal; we live such easy, safe and even comfortable Christian lives. Some of this is due to our own weak witness and compromise with the world around us, but much of it is due, in the providence of God, to easier times for the Church in these democracies than most of the earlier believers knew. In these days, for us at least, persecution is the exception and freedom the norm; in New Testament times it was, for many, the other way around! Elsewhere in the world, under totalitarian régimes, secular and religious, Christian believers in the twentieth century have suffered as much as their first-century brothers and sisters.

The Greek word for a witness, as in a court of law, was *martus* from which we get our word martyr. So many of the early witnesses to Christ paid for their testimony with their life that the word became a technical term for just that. At the end of our chapter the author groups together 'the noble army of martyrs' as those who 'refused to be released, so that they might gain a better resurrection' (Heb 11:35). After mentioning those like David and the judges who 'through faith conquored kingdoms and administered justice' and gained what they had been promised in evident success against their enemies, he goes on to indicate other unnamed examples of faith who overcame opposition and were vindicated in their day (Heb 11:33–5). The reference to Daniel in Babylon is clear in the phrase 'who shut the mouths of lions' as is the reference to Shadrach, Mishach and Abednego in 'quenched the fury of the flames'. The ministries of Elijah and Elisha are clearly in mind when he refers to women who 'received back their dead, raised to life again' (1 Kgs 17:17–24; 2 Kgs 4:8–37).

The climax of his argument, however, is reserved for those who did not experience vindication or deliverance on earth:

> Others were tortured and refused to be released, so that they might gain a better resurrection. Some faced jeers and flogging, while others were chained and put in prison. They were stoned, they were sawn in two; they were put to death by the sword. They went about in sheepskins and goatskins, destitute, persecuted and ill-treated – the world was not worthy of them. They wandered in deserts and mountains and in caves and holes in the ground (Heb 11:36–8)

These all had the opportunity to gain their freedom and ensure earthly peace for themselves, but at the price of renouncing their faith. It was a price they steadfastly refused to pay.

The first example he chooses would have been well known to every Jew, though it is not in our Old Testament. Commentators generally agree that the reference in verse 35 to those who were 'tortured and refused to be released so that they might gain a better resurrection' was meant to recall the heroic resistance of the Maccabean days only a little over two hundred years earlier. F.F. Bruce writes:

> The particular form of torture indicated by the Greek verb is being stretched on the rack and beaten to death. This was precisely the punishment meted out to Eleazar, one of the noble confessors of Maccabean days who willingly accepted death rather than foreswear his loyalty to God. In 2 Maccabees the story of his martyrdom is followed by the record of the mother and her seven sons who endured this and other forms of torture

195

rather than transgress the law of God. In this story one brother after another declares his readiness to accept torture and death because of the hope of resurrection.[1]

One says to the king, 'You accursed wretch, you dismiss us from this present life, but the King of the universe will raise us up to an everlasting renewal of life, because we have died for his laws' (2 Macc 7:9). Another holds out his limbs to be mutilated saying 'I got these from heaven and because of his laws I disdain them, and from him I hope to get them back again' (2 Macc 7:11). A third brother at the point of death says, 'One cannot but choose to die at the hands of men and to cherish the hope that God gives of being raised again by him. But for you there will be no resurrection to life'! (2 Macc 7:14).[2]

Of whom the world was not worthy

It seems likely that the writer of Hebrews in the verse that follows (Heb 11:36) is referring to Jeremiah, who was beaten and put in the stocks (Jer 20:2) and made an object of mockery (Jer 20:7f). Some time later he was again beaten and put in prison (Jer 37:15; 38:6f). Jewish tradition has it that he was finally stoned to death by his own countrymen down in Egypt, where he had been taken after the fall of Jerusalem, enraged because of his protest against their continuing idolatry. Jesus himself speaks of the fate of the priest-prophet Zachariah who was stoned to death at the instigation of King Joash (2 Chr 24:21).

Jewish tradition claimed that the prophet Isaiah was 'sawn in two' in the evil reign of Manasseh, and while some, like Elijah in the time of Jezebel, survived (1 Kgs 19:18), many were 'put to death by the sword' (Heb 11:37, cf. Kgs 19:10). William Lane comments:

Although the call to the prophetic office did not always entail a violent death, it often meant a life of severe privation. This aspect of faith is exposed in v. 37b: 'they went about in sheepskins and goatskins destitute, oppressed and mistreated.' ... The allusion is primarily to Elijah and Elisha ... The hairy cloak appears to have become the standard uniform of the prophets (Zech 13:4). The writer finds in the characteristic garb of the prophets a symbol of their distinctiveness from the world and of their impoverished condition.[3]

Many who like them were faithful in times of persecution took flight to the hill country or deserts of Palestine and lived with great hardship and danger 'in caves and holes in the ground' (Heb 11:38). 'These were all commended for their faith,' says our writer, they lived off the promises of God all their lives, 'yet none of them received what had been promised' (v.39). They had to wait and not only live but also die without receiving what had been promised. This was not because God could not be trusted but because he had 'planned something better' (v.40) than anything they had conceived of or looked forward to 'so that only together with us would they be made perfect' or 'brought to perfection'. That perfection is our common future in Christ 'who is the end of the law' (Rom 10:4; Heb 10:1–9), the once-for-all sacrifice for sin (Heb 10:10–14), the summit of God's purposes and the fullness of the Church of God.

In Christ the whole Church of God past and present reaches its perfection. 'It is unnecessary,' says William Lane, 'to distinguish here between the achievement of Christ at his first coming and the full realisation of God's promises at the Second Coming.'[4] His sacrificial death is the basis of their and our acceptance with God (Heb 9:15) and his Second Coming will be the glory and fulfilment of all that for which they hoped and endured so much (Heb 9:27; 12:28).

The Hebrew Christians reading this epistle need to see themselves as occupying a high point in the purposes of God and to stand firm to the end in that knowledge. The great examples of faith in suffering come from an era which did not yet know Christ in the flesh or the truth in its fullness. John Calvin writes:

If those on whom the great light of grace had not yet shone showed such surpassing constancy in bearing their ills, what effect ought the full glory of the gospel to have on us? A tiny spark led them to heaven, but now the Son of righteousness shines on us what excuse shall we offer if we still cling to the earth?[5]

Avoidable sufferings

There are important lessons for us in all this. When we read of 'trials' we too often forget the implication of the word which is not calamity but proof as, for instance, where we speak of a new car or aeroplane being put through its 'trials'. God never gave us faith as an ornament but as a working tool, a piece of equipment to be used in battle, something that can take hard knocks and the heat of trying situations.

We often apply certain New Testament passages on suffering, for example those on carrying our cross (Mt 10:38, 39), on rejoicing in our sufferings (Rom 5:3–5; Jas 1:2–4) or on God as the God of all comfort (2 Cor 1:3), to sickness or misfortune or the onset of age, etc., but the references there are not simply to sufferings as such. We are all vulnerable to life's pain and loss, but there the references are to *avoidable sufferings*: carrying a cross we do not have to shoulder and which we take up only because we are followers of the Christ who said, 'If anyone would come after me, he must deny himself and take up his cross and follow me' (Mt 16:24).

That cross can be refused or even put down at any time and at a price we can purchase immunity from the world's dislike and even gain its favour (Mt 16:25–6), but even if we gain the whole world the price is fearful and the respite short (Mt 16:26–7). The Apostle Paul wrote to Timothy: 'Everyone who wants to live a godly live will be persecuted' (2 Tim 3:12).

It is impossible to live the Christian life without such conflict: areas of conflict will appear in faith and lifestyle, in the world and even in the Church, in religion, economics, politics, social life and working life. Of course if your godliness is a private or weekend thing, then it will not get you into any trouble; it is then 'privately engaging but socially irrelevent', as Os Guinness remarks.[6] But let it be applied to the world at large, in the workplace and the week, and it will bring you into conflict very soon with dishonesty, exploitation, prejudice and self-seeking. We are anointed for conflict, peace-makers though we may be. We do not have to look for it, it will soon come to us if we are faithful.

Above everything else it is the call and the warning of the gospel that brings us into trouble in the world. When the young Saul of Tarsus was called to witness to Christ in the ancient world, he was shown how much he was destined to suffer for Christ (Acts 9:16). Thirteen years later his back was a map of those sufferings, criss-crossed with the marks of whippings and beatings. Hence he could say to the Galatians: 'Finally let no one cause me trouble for I bear on my body the marks of Jesus' (Gal 6:17; cf. 2 Cor 6:4–10; 11:23–7).

How should we respond to such sufferings in our own lives? Those sufferings may not (yet?) be in extreme forms and we must not be unrealistic or merely 'romantic' in our attitudes. Someone once asked the great Victorian evangelist and preacher C.H. Spurgeon, 'Are you prepared to burn at the stake for your faith like the martyrs you so often refer to, Mr Spurgeon?' The great preacher, never less than honest but with great practical wisdom replied: 'Well, since you ask me, sitting in this chair so comfortably, I do not think I can confidently say that I am. However, I believe if the time came when I should be faced with the choice, I would be given grace to burn for my Saviour.'

Consider it pure joy

Perhaps the most striking feature of the real-life experiences of persecution in the New Testament and in the exhortation of its writers is the consistent element of joy that appears. From the early days of the young Church's persecution we read: 'The apostles left the Sanhedrin, rejoicing because they had been counted worthy of suffering disgrace for the Name' (Acts 5.41). When Paul and Silas were in the jail at Philippi, they sang hymns, even after a severe flogging (Acts 16:23-5).

For Richard Wurmbrandt, the Romanian pastor, alone in his cell, cold, hungry and in rags, yet dancing for joy every night, the words of another apostle, himself destined for martyrdom and writing to a suffering church, have proved true:

> In this you greatly rejoice, though now for a little while you may have had to suffer grief in all kinds of trials. These have come so that your faith – of greater worth than gold, which perishes even though refined by fire may be proved genuine and may result in praise, glory and honour when Jesus Christ is revealed. Though you have not seen him, you love him, and even though you do not see him now, you believe in him and are filled with an inexpressible and glorious joy, for you are receiving the goal of your faith, the salvation of your souls (1 Pet 1:6-9, cf. Jas 1:2-4.)

Very many of these 'refused to be released' at the price of denying their faith 'so that they might gain a better resurrection'. But the crown they won was 'a crown that will last forever' (1 Cor 9:25; 2 Tim 4:8).

A few years ago my wife Valerie and I spent an unforgettable day in the ruins of old Corinth in Greece. It was fascinating to pace out the old city, to decipher its transcriptions, to reconstruct its shape and size, to stand in the remains of its shops and to peer in at the 'Pierian spring' that Milton waxed lyrical about (pretty disappointing actually, in its dank and dismal cavern!). The most fascinating moments came when we stood before the high platform of earth and stone, the *bema* from which the Roman governor judged prisoners and other matters. Paul had been hauled before Gallio on that very spot (Acts 18:12-17). Then Gallio had been everything and Paul nothing. But who now remembers the Roman governor, though millions in the Church know his Christian prisoner?

Where is Gallio now – and where is Paul? I was so struck by these thoughts that I stood on the platform itself holding aloft a New Testament open at Acts chapter 18 while my wife took a photograph of the scene! When we both explored the platform more thoroughly, we found there a large block of stone and on it some words of Paul written to the Corinthian believers a short time later. They are the epitaph we can write for all the heroes and martyrs of Hebrew chapter 11: 'For our light and momentary troubles are achieving for us an eternal glory that far outweighs them all' (2 Cor 4:18). That is a faith to live by and it is a faith we can die by too.

24

FAITH LOOKING UNTO JESUS

Therefore, since we are surrounded by such a great cloud of witnesses, let us throw off everything that hinders and the sin that so easily entangles, and let us run with perseverance the race marked out for us. Let us fix our eyes on Jesus, the author and perfector of our faith, who for the joy set before him endured the cross, scorning its shame, and sat down at the right hand of the throne of God. Consider him who endured such opposition from sinful men, so that you will not grow weary and lose heart. (Heb 12:1–2.)

It's well known that when, in reading the Bible, you come across a 'therefore' you should look and see what it's there for! This first word in the twelfth chapter of Hebrews links it (and us) to the great figures of chapter 11. It tells us that their histories are there for a purpose, and we are part of that purpose. They are part of our story and, indeed, we are part of theirs (Heb 11:40). Paul tells the Roman Christians: 'Everything that was written in the past was written to teach us, so that through endurance and the encouragement of the Scriptures, we might have hope' (Rom 15:4).

When we become Christians, Christ brings us into a new society – a family extended in space and time: the Church of today and yesterday. He who makes all things new gives us new lives with relationships, new standards and new priorities. He gives us new role models too: people like Abel, the first martyr who lost favour with man but found favour with God; Enoch, who enjoyed a lonely but privileged walk with God; Abraham, who left an earthly city for a heavenly one; Moses, who preferred to be a friend of God than a prince of Egypt; Joseph and Joshua, David and Samuel and the prophets, whose glory was God. Their lives are meant to speak to us, to encourage us, to challenge us and to remind us where we most truly belong. These people are more relevant and more real than any galaxy of stars on our TV or cinema screens. They offer substantial and life-long help in facing life's challenges and crises. They lived and overcame by faith and so, they tell us, can we.

In the stadium

The picture suggested in verse 1 is of a sports stadium in the ancient world. There on the stone seats rising up tier after tier are a great company of believers who lived in our world in the times before Christ came. In the middle of the stadium are the Christians, their spiritual heirs in the new era, the era of the new covenant.

So we have the heroes of the past urging on the contestants of the present: Abraham calling out encouragement to those who have to wait long for the promises of God to be fulfilled; Moses comforting those who have surrendered wealth or career, comfort or reputation and esteem for the call of God to better things; the martyrs, named and unnamed, who whisper encouragement in the ears of those who suffer *without* deliverance in this world. We too are in the same arena of faith with the same opportunity that they had, and the same call to 'run in such a way as to get the prize' (1 Cor 9:24).

The metaphor of a sports stadium and its races to illustrate the demands of the moral and ethical life was a common one in the ancient world. It is often used by the Apostle Paul to illustrate and enforce the demands of discipleship. He uses it to good effect in writing to the Corinthian church, a church which was relaxing in the Spirit when it should have been wrestling in the world (1 Cor 9:24–7). In his last epistle he clearly sees himself in the stadium as one who has 'finished the race' by living the life of faith (2 Tim 4:7). Here the writer to the Hebrews similarly envisages 'the games' – but what he writes about is no game.

The unhindered Christian

The first thing the runners did as they approached the starting blocks was to take off their clothes (they ran naked in those days). Our writer uses this when he writes: 'Let us lay aside anything that hinders' or 'Let us lay aside all excess weight.' William Lane writes:

> The term occurs only here in biblical Greek but had been used metaphorically of vices since the time of Demosthenes. Here it refers more naturally to the weight of a long heavy robe which would hamper running; it may apply equally to superfluous bodily weight ... The combined expression covers any encumberance that would handicap a runner, and by analogy anything that would interfere with responsible commitment to Jesus Christ.[1]

He cites such examples as love of wealth, attachment to the world, preoccupation with earthly interests, or self-importance.

God wants the believer to be unhindered in the great race. The unhindered Christian is not one without job or wife or children, nor is it someone who has turned their back upon company, enjoyments or responsibilities; it is one who has dispensed with things that hindered their walk with God: things that could not be sanctified. Are there things in your life that are expertly 'excused' but cannot be sanctified? Are you running a race with a suitcase in your hand and a backpack on your shoulders, hanging on to wrong loyalties, habits, priorities, pride, selfishness, fears and other excess baggage?

The Authorised Version and the Revised Standard Version give the rendering: 'Let us lay aside every weight.' Obviously there are weights in life that have to be carried: family responsibilities, compassionate service and even sickness, handicap and age. However, the 'weight' here is sin. Sin is always a weight. We've all seen astonishing feats of strength in weight-lifting contests or 'the strongest man in the world' contests, but no one imagines that anyone could run a race carrying such weights or that they could be held up for long or carried far.

Yet our society encourages us in the foolish belief that we can sin and get away with it, that we can cheat on our employer or partner and not have to carry the consequences. But we do have to carry the consequences, often a crippling load of them, and they are not easily shed – if shed at all. When God comes into our lives with forgiveness, freedom and new power to live for him, when he lifts the burdens and give us a new start, we are fools indeed if we begin to pick up new burdens, secret sins, unwarranted entanglements. Sooner or later they will trip us up, exhaust us with their weight, or in some other way attack us in our pride.

The undistracted Christian

Our translation speaks of sin 'that so easily entangles'. William Lane, however, learnedly argues for a translation here which differs slightly from others and renders an alternative Greek reading: the sin which is 'liable to distract' (cf. NEB margin – 'the sin which all too readily distracts us') and writes:

Christians are always capable of being subverted by 'the deceitful attractiveness of sin' (Heb 3:13b). One has only to reflect upon everyday compromises of faith in an effort to avoid conflict or to conform to the norms of society at large. The writer warns his audience to guard against sin in any form because it will distract them, causing them to look away when they should be fixing their gaze upon Jesus. (Heb 12:2.)[2]

I sometimes illustrate this danger by telling the old Greek story of Atalanta and the golden apples. Atalanta was beautiful and suitors for her hand were many. She was also athletic and very fast in the race, so her would-be lovers were challenged to a race for her hand in marriage. If they won the race they won her also; however, if they lost they forfeited their lives. The judge of the race was one Hippomenes. In spite of the fact that many failed and died for their temerity, Hippomenes too, eventually, came under the spell of her beauty. Hippomenes offered himself for the contest and the prize, but first he sought and obtained help from Aphrodite, the goddess of love. She gave him three golden apples with instructions about what to do.

As the race began, Atalanta was so confident that she gave Hippomenes a head start before she herself shot from the starting line. They skimmed over the sand at the shoreline and Atalanta began to gain. Then Hippomenes threw down one of his golden apples and Atalanta, startled but curious, stopped to pick it up. He sped on but she soon gained and he threw to one side his second golden apple. Full of confidence in her ability to make up the lost time she stopped once more to pick up the bauble. A third time she gained on him and a third time he threw a golden apple down. Unable to resist Atalanta stopped yet again, picked it up and ran on. This time however they were too near the finishing line for her to catch him up and Hippomenes won both the race and Atalanta's hand (personally, I wouldn't have gone anywhere near her, but there is, as they say, no accounting for taste!).

The golden apples defeated her as they have defeated many. What are the golden apples in your life distracting you, alluring you, hindering you? Ambition? Pride? Materialism? Lust? Are there things which are taking your eyes off Christ your Saviour and your Lord? Are you stopping in the marathon, not through exhaustion but out of fascination? Fix your gaze upon Jesus, consider his infinitely superior beauty and truth and worth. In such a context the words of the old song come into their own:

> Turn your eyes upon Jesus
> Look full in his wonderful face
> That the things of earth may grow strangely dim
> In the light of his glory and grace.

Jesus is at the finishing line, indeed, his arms *are* the finishing line. Let us run right on into them!

The glory of going on

'And let us run with perseverance the race marked out for us' (Heb 12:1). The word here translated 'perseverance' is rendered 'endurance' in verses 2 and 3. Endurance is a key concept throughout this passage (Heb 12:1–13). The race marked out for us is not an easy one; it is not a sprint but a marathon; the essential quality is staying power. It calls for commitment, hard training and stamina. Philip Hughes notes:

> One of the chief problems with the Hebrew Christians to whom this letter is addressed is that they have set out on the race, but after a good start (Heb 10:32–4) are now slackening in the will to persevere; their effort is decreasing (2:1), sin is holding them back (3:17–4:1), they need to recover their intensity of purpose (4:11), to shake off the sluggish mood into which they have fallen (6:11f), to regain their confidence (10:35, 39) and their competitive spirit (12:12).[3]

We too tend to tire after a good start, to forget the privilege of being *in* the race, to forget the 'cloud of witnesses' and even the prize. We complain of the heat, the distractions, the discomforts and feel little of the excitement of the starting tape, the first days of our conversion. We need to recognise the glory of going on! Sometimes the Christian life is downhill with a bright sky and a following wind but at other times the track winds steeply upwards, sharp stones dig into our feet and there seems no one to cheer us on. At such times we are called only to keep going; not to sing but to slog. However, at those times and at all times we are to run the race 'looking unto Jesus' (AV).

Looking unto Jesus

'Let us fix our eyes on Jesus' (Heb 12:2). Here the writer uses a verb (Greek *aphoraō*) which signifies to look away from the immediate surroundings. His idea is of a concentrated attention that turns away from all distractions and fixes its gaze on Jesus. It is interesting to see how the idea of *looking* recurs again and again in chapters 11 and 12. Abraham 'looked' to the city which has foundations (Heb 11:10; Greek *ekdexomai*, to expect, to look for and wait for); Moses 'looked' to the reward (11:26; Greek *apoblepō*, to look away from one thing to another) and 'kept on looking' (the verb is in the imperfect tense) through the Midian years to the invisible God and persevered 'as seeing' him who is invisible (better rendered by Lane 'kept the one who is invisible continually before his eyes').[4]

So also we must keep on looking not at faith's discouragements or distractions but at Jesus. The simple use of Jesus' name suggests that it is his humanity which is to be considered here and the context of enduring indicates his earthly sufferings in which he stands as an incomparable example of faithful endurance. They are to consider chiefly his 'obedience unto death' (Phil 2:8b), but many other sufferings prepared him for Calvary. He was resented at Nazareth, hated by the religious leaders, slandered by some, used by others, misunderstood in his own family and scarcely understood by his own disciples. After three years of ministry he was betrayed, judged and crucified by wicked and lawless men. Yet in all this our writer sees him as 'the author and perfector of our faith'.

Jesus as champion

'The author and perfecter of our faith' (Heb 12:2). In the context of a sports arena we would do better to translate 'author' (Greek *archegos*) as 'champion'. Lane renders the whole line: 'the champion in the exercise of faith and the one who brought faith to complete expression'.[5]

Against the tendency of the usual temptations he stresses that 'faith' here is not *our* faith perfected by Jesus but 'faith' absolutely considered. Jesus is the one in whom faith has reached its perfection. He is the supreme exponent of faith. Philip Hughes puts it well:

> The incarnate Son is himself the man of faith *par excellence* ... His whole earthly life is the very embodiment of trust in God (Heb 2:13). It is marked from start to finish by total dependance on the Father and complete attunement to his will' (Heb 10:7–10).[6]

Jesus lived a life of faith as no one has ever lived it. Abraham lied and Moses sinned, David committed adultery and murder, Gideon and Samson were flawed models but Jesus did nothing without the Father's will and always did what pleased the one who sent him. From Bethlehem to Calvary his life was an unbroken obedience, a seamless robe of righteousness. That righteousness is now God's gift to sinners, for Christ is our righteousness (Rom 1:17; 1 Cor 1:30; 2 Cor 5:21) and our foundation (1 Cor 3:11). Which is why we can follow him for he will not let us down any more than he let God his Father down. He is our champion.

Jesus in shame and glory

'Who for the joy set before him endured the cross, scorning its shame, and sat down at the right hand of the throne of God' (Heb 12:2). There have always been two different interpretations of the first part of this. The word 'for' in the phrase 'for the joy set before him' is the Greek word *anti* which in biblical Greek nearly always means 'instead of' but may in a few places (e.g. Mt 17:7; Eph 5:31; Heb 11:16) mean 'for the sake of' (as it often does in classical Greek). If the first translation is the right one (as Lane argues) the writer of Hebrews would be referring back to our Lord's decision in his preincarnate life in the

Godhead to come into this world to die *instead of* remaining in the glory and joy of heaven (cf. Phil 2: 6–7).

However, Hughes argues that the second translation better suits the context and indeed it does seem more natural to think of the joy which was 'set before him' as something he did not yet have. It was the vision of the Father's house, the Father's joy and our own final salvation which sustained him, including the last great day when he would present the Church of the redeemed, complete and glorified, to his Father saying, 'Here am I, and the children God has given me' (Heb 2:13).

No doubt Jesus, in his earthly life and ministry, meditated a great deal on Isaiah 53, including the words: 'After the suffering of his soul, he will see the light of life and be satisfied' (Is 53:11). Surely in all the Scriptures that spoke of him (Lk 24:27) it was the final servant-song of Isaiah that was best fitted to help him endure the cross with all its pain and shame.

In Roman times it was the rule to nail the victim by both hands and feet (binding the victim to the cross only with bonds was the exception). Crucifixion could serve as a 'popular entertainment' but the cultured literary world of Rome found it an embarrassing as well as a horrific business and rarely referred to it. John Stott writes in *The Cross of Christ*:

> It is probably the most cruel method of execution ever practised, for it deliberately delayed death until maximum torture had been inflicted. The victim could suffer for days before dying. While the Romans adopted it, they reserved it for criminals convicted of murder, rebellion or armed robbery, provided that they were also slaves, foreigners or other non-persons ... Roman citizens were exempt from crucifixion, except in extreme cases of treason. Cicero in one of his speeches condemned it as 'a most cruel and disgusting punishment.'[7]

Martin Hengel tells us that someone condemned to crucifixion was seen as now having no human rights of any sort, and could be tortured by the soldiers in any way while on the cross or beforehand.[8]

The readers of Hebrews are to fix their eyes on Jesus when under threat and in times of suffering. He stands before them not only as an incomparable example but as a once-for-all atoning sacrifice (Heb 9 and 10). He suffered untold pain and unimaginable horrors bearing not only the malice of man but the wrath of God due to sin (Gal 3:13; cf. Rom 3:25; 2 Cor 5:21). Yet, scorning the shame of the one and submitting utterly to the will of the Father in the other (Jn 12:24, 27–8), he endured and has now 'sat down at the right hand of the throne of God' (cf. Heb 1:3).

There, at the right hand of God, the place of majesty and power, he lives, and not for himself alone. By his intercessory life for us (Heb 7:25) he lives to do more than watch and encourage us, he lives to guard us and empower us, he runs alongside us in our race and he will give us the crown of victory at its end (1 Cor 9:4, 25; 2 Tim 4:7–8) which he purchased for us with his blood before ever we ran for it in faith. Jesus is not simply the crowning example of faith but the one and only Saviour of those who have faith.

These persecuted believers, despised by their own Jewish people as renegades as well as by the pagans, are to 'consider him who endured such opposition from sinful men' so that they might not grow weary 'and lose heart' (Heb 12:3). Jesus scorned the shame of his cruel and unjust treatment and God reversed the verdict of men by raising him from the dead and giving him a unique place in the divine glory (Acts 2:32–3, 36). Now his followers must be prepared to share his disgrace but their profound comfort and reassurance will come from considering the glory he has entered and promised to them: 'Let us then go to him outside the camp, bearing the disgrace he bore. For here we do not have an enduring city, but we are looking for the city that is to come' (Heb 13:13–14).

Our study thus leaves us looking up and looking forward to a glory which we shall share with 'the spirits of

212

just men and women made perfect' and above all with the Lord they served and with the Lamb who is, with his Father, the light and glory of the city of God. That is our destiny and the destiny of all the people of God in every age from the greatest to the least. On that day none shall be forgotten and no one will be obscure as Christ presents the completed Church to the Father and says 'Here am I, and the children God has given me' (Heb 2:13).

The nineteenth-century preacher C. H. Spurgeon often sent books from his library to their authors asking for their signature and a photograph. One of them, the godly Scot, Andrew Bonar, wrote back: 'Dear brother, I cannot refuse what you are so kind to ask. But if you had only waited a little while, it would have been really worth having – for "we shall be LIKE HIM"' (1 John 3:2).[9]

We cannot begin to imagine either the glory he has or the glory he has waiting for us (1 Cor 1:9) notwithstanding all our studies. As one of the greatest of our older English theologians, the puritan divine John Owen, has put it: 'We may suppose that we have here attained great knowledge, clear and high thoughts of God; but alas! when he shall bring us into his presence we shall cry out, "We never knew him as he is; the thousandth part of his glory and perfection, and blessedness, never entered into our hearts."'[10]

NOTES

Chapter 1   Celebration of Faith

1 *See* Nigel Hawkes, 'The Greatest discovery of all time?'. *The Times*, 2 May 1994, p. 7
2 Ibid.
3 *The Times*, 11 May 1994, Letters.
4 E. Käsemann in *Word Biblical Commentary*, Vol 47B, 'Hebrews 9–13' by William L. Lane (Word Books, Dallas, 1991), p. 328
5 Lane, ibid, p. 329
6 John Calvin *Institutes of the Christian Religion*, ed. John T. McNeill (Westminster Press, Philadelphia), Bk III, ch 1, sects 1–4
7 Calvin, op. cit., Bk III, ch ii, sect 7

Chapter 2   Faith Recognising Its Creator

1 A. van den Beukel, *More things in heaven and earth: God and the Scientist* (SCM, London, 1991), ch 2 nl, p. 86
2 Brian Appleyard, *Understanding the Present: Science and the Soul of Man* (Picador, Pan, London, 1993), p. 16
3 Ibid, p. xiv
4 Ibid., p. 14
5 Ibid., p. 249
6 Joseph Hart (1712–68), 'How good is the God we adore'
7 Thomas Seiger Derr, 'Geology and Liberation: a Theological Critique of the Use and Abuse of our Birthright' (WSCE, Geneva), p. 19

Chapter 3   Faith Resented and Honoured

1 Walter Brueggemann, *Genesis* (John Knox Press, Atlanta, 1982), p. 55

Chapter 4　Faith Walking with God

1 David F. Wells, *God in the Wasteland* (Erdmans, Grand Rapids/IVP, Leicester, 1994), p. 11

Chapter 5　Faith and Its Reward

1 Aldous Huxley, *Ends and Means* (HarperCollins), quoted in Michael Green, *World on the Run* (IVP, Leicester, 1983), p. 62
2 Lane, op. cit., p. 338
3 Philip Edgcumbe Hughes, *A Commentary on the Epistle to the Hebrews* (Erdmans, Grand Rapids, 1977), p. 461
4 Martin Bucer, 'A Brief Summary of Christian Doctrine', 10 (1548), quoted in Hughes, op. cit., p. 461
5 St Augustine, *De Gratia et Libero Arbitris*, 15, 17, quoted in Hughes, op. cit., p. 461
6 J. I. Packer and Thomas Howard, *Christianity: the True Humanism* (Word Publishing, Berkhamstead, 1985), pp. 102, 103

Chapter 6　Faith Learning to Fear

1 Eccesiasticus 44
2 See, for example, the article 'Flood' in *The International Standard Bible Encyclopaedia*, ed. Bromily (Eerdmans, Grand Rapids, 1982), vol 2, pp. 315–21; and Victor P. Hamilton, *The Book of Genesis* (Eerdmans, Grand Rapids, 1990), ch 1–17, pp. 272–330
3 Alexander Maclaren (1826–1910), *Maclaren's Exposition of Holy Scripture* (Eerdmans, Grand Rapids, 1952), Vol 1, p. 53
4 Maclaren, op. cit., Vol 10, p. 114

Chapter 7　Faith Aware of Its Inheritance

1 Joseph Parker (1830–1902), 'God holds the key of all unknown'
2 James Montgomery (1771–1854), 'For ever with the Lord'

Chapter 8　Faith Grasping the Promises of God

1 C. H. Spurgeon (1834–92), *The Metropolitan Tabernacle Pulpit* (Pilgrim Publications, Pasadena, 1977), Vol 46, p. 19

Chapter 9   Faith Looking Forward

1 Lane, op. cit., pp. 345, 356
2 Philip Edgcumbe Hughes, op. cit., p. 477
3 From the second-century anonymous *Epistle to Diognetus*, 5, 9

Chapter 10   Faith Tested and Triumphant

1 Frederick Langbridge (1849–1923), *A Cluster of Quiet Thoughts* (1896) (Religious Tract Society pubn)
2 Lane, op. cit., p. 360
3 Hughes, op. cit., pp. 483, 486
4 Cecil Frances Alexander, (1818–95) 'There is a green hill far away'
5 Gordon J. Wenham, *Word Biblical Commentary*, Vol 2, 'Genesis 16–50' (Word Books, Dallas, 1994), p. 116

Chapter 12   Faith Making Its Choice

1 P. T. Forsyth, *The Justification of God* (Duckworth, 1916), quoted in John Stott, *The Cross of Christ* (IVP, Leicester, 1986), p. 336
2 Alan Cole, *Exodus: an introduction and commentary* (IVP, Leicester, 1973), pp. 57–8
3 G. A. F. Knight, *Theology as Narrative* (The Handsel Press Ltd, Edinburgh, 1976), p. 8
4 Os Guinness, *The Grave-digger File* (IVP, Leicester, 1983), p. 12
5 C. S. Lewis, *The Screwtape Letters* (Various editions), Letter 13

Chapter 13   Faith Taking Shelter in God

1 Donald Bridge, *Signs and Wonders Today* (IVP, Leicester, 1985), p. 17
2 Ibid., p. 59
3 G. H. C. MacGregor quoted in *The Gospel of John*, by L. Morris, New International Commentary (Eerdmans, Grand Rapids, 1973), p. 362
4 Gordon J. Wenham, *The Book of Leviticus, New International Commentary* (Eerdmans, Grand Rapids, 1979), pp. 19, 20
5 Ibid., pp. 22, 26, 55
6 Calvin, op. cit., Bk III, ch ii, sect 7
7 Charles Wesley (1707–88), 'And can it be'

Chapter 14   Faith Passing the Point of No Return

1 Alan Cole, op. cit., p. 121
2 G. A. F. Knight, op. cit., pp. 104, 105
3 Ibid., p. 106
4 John Owen (1616–83), *An Exposition of Hebrews* (Sovereign Grace Publishers, Evansville 13, Indiana, 1960), Vol VII, p. 170
5 John Calvin, *The Epistle of Paul the Apostle to the Hebrews*, ed. Torrance (Eerdmans, Grand Rapids, 1979), p. 180

Chapter 15   Faith Aware of God's Power

1 John Owen, op. cit., p. 177

Chapter 16   Faith Taking its Opportunities

1 S. Cohon and N. J. Opperwall, 'Barak' in *The International Standard Bible Encyclopaedia* (Eerdmans, Grand Rapids), Vol 1, p. 430
2 Arthur E. Cundall, *Judges* (The Tyndale Press, London, 1968) pp. 86–8
3 Os Guinness, *Doubt: Faith in two minds* (Lion Publishing, Tring, 1979), p. 204
4 Cundall, op. cit., p. 88
5 William Shakespeare, *Julius Caesar*, IV, ii. 217

Chapter 17   Faith Learning to Fight

1 John White and Ken Blue, *Healing the Wounded: the costly love of church discipline* (IVP, Leicester, 1985), p. 34
2 C. H. Spurgeon, op. cit., Vol. 31 (1885), p. 651

Chapter 18   Faith Rising Above Rejection

1 John Bunyan (1628–88), 'He who would valiant be'
2 C. F. Keil and F. Delitzch, *Commentary on the Old Testament* in 10 vols (Eerdmans, n.d.), Vol 2, pp. 388–95
3 Leon Wood, *Distressing Days of the Judges* (Zondervan, Grand Rapids, 1976), pp. 287–95

Chapter 19   Faith Learning the Hard Way

1 John Milton (1608–74), *Samson Agonistes*, 1. 41

Chapter 22   Faith Losing Control

1 Lois Mowday, *The Snare* (Nav Press, Reading, 1988), pp. 84, 90

2 Ewald Plass, *This is Luther* (Concordia, St Louis, 1958), pp. 91, 92

3 Fanny J. Crosby (1820–1915), 'To God be the Glory'

Chapter 23   Faith Suffering

1 F. F. Bruce, op. cit., pp. 337, 338

2 Ibid., p. 338

3 William L. Lane, op. cit., p. 391

4 Ibid., p. 393

5 Calvin quoted in Hughes, op. cit., p. 516

6 Theodore Roszak, *Where the Wasteland Ends* (Doubleday, New York, 1973), p. 449, quoted in Os Guinness, *The Gravedigger File* (IVP, Leicester, 1983), pp. 81, 82

Chapter 24   Faith Looking Unto Jesus

1 Lane, op. cit., p. 409

2 Ibid

3 Hughes, op. cit., p. 520

4 Lane, op. cit., pp. 367, 375, 376

5 Ibid., pp. 397, 411

6 Hughes, op. cit., p. 522

7 John Stott, *The Cross of Christ* (IVP, Leicester, 1986), pp. 23, 24

8 Martin Hengel, *The Cross of the Son of God* (SCM, London, 1986), pp. 117f

9 C. H. Spurgeon's Autobiography (Passmore and Alabaster, London, 1900), Vol IV, pp. 297, 298

10 *The Works of John Owen*, ed. Goold (Banner of Truth, Edinburgh, 1977), Vol VI, p. 65